Empaths are
Dancers Between Realms
carrying a quiet song of
receptivity and responsiveness
in a world that can be
loud, harsh and insensitive.

DANCERS BETWEEN REALMS

Empath Energy
Beyond Empathy

Dancers Between Realms –
Empath Energy, *Beyond Empathy*

ISBN **978-0-944370-01-8**

Library of Congress Control Number: 2006904776

Spiritual Psychology

This book was developed and produced by

Synchronicity Press

Box 1154

Waynesboro, VA 22980

www.synchronicitypress.com

Synchronicity - the sense of significance beyond chance

Cover Design & Author Photo
by Leslie France
www.bluewebweaver.com

Cover Image by Deb Booth
www.differentlightstudio.com

Printed in the United States of America

DANCERS BETWEEN REALMS

Empath Energy
Beyond Empathy

Elisabeth Y. Fitzhugh

First Edition
2006

SYNCHRONICITY PRESS

Waynesboro, Virginia

You are dancing in a
great realm of discovery.
It is part of the gift of your time.
Life is supporting your journey of
dancing between realms.

CONTENTS

A CONTENT NOTE I

INTRODUCTION II

CHAPTER ONE

   UNDERSTANDING YOURSELF AS AN EMPATH 1

CHAPTER TWO

   TOOLS AND TECHNIQUES OF AWARENESS 21

CHAPTER THREE

   ON RELATING 41

CHAPTER FOUR

   IN RELATIONSHIP 73

CHAPTER FIVE

   DANCING WITH THE PHYSICAL 91

CHAPTER SIX

   CHILDREN AND CHILDHOOD 109

CHAPTER SEVEN

   SHARING THROUGH QUESTIONS AND ANSWERS 127

CHAPTER EIGHT

   INTRODUCTION TO GLOSSARY 159

   GLOSSARY OF PRINCIPLES AND TOOLS 162

ACKNOWLEDGMENTS 178

ABOUT THE AUTHOR 180

We attract the information we need to awaken
the conscious mind, the inner mind,
the expansive mind for growth.

Your own discernment will lead you to that which is
most useful and supportive to you.

Your willingness to listen, question and look still
once again, will lead you on a ever fresh,
continuing journey of discovery.

This book is a dance of collaboration over years of exploring the empath material. The majority of material in this book has been compiled, excerpted and edited from transcribed audio tapes of workshops and personal sessions. As a result, the text at times moves from a personal, one-to-one voice to a third-person voice.

The book also includes additional text written directly for this edition. Throughout, stylized quotes highlight aspects of the material and can be used as reference markers. A useful glossary of the many principles and tools explored throughout the book is also included.

The names and details of participants have been changed for confidentiality. Some quoted questions have been edited. The context and sequence of some questions have been modified. All material is used with permission of the participants and edited or written by Elisabeth Y. Fitzhugh.

INTRODUCTION

The Empath. The word has found its way into our consciousness — accompanied by ideas of sharing and healing emotion and pain. There are vivid iconic images such as the empath episode of the original Star Trek © television series, in which the alien empath must overcome her own fear of pain and death to come into accepting her nature as a healer. Star Trek again explores empath nature, with the character of Deanna Troi, as an empath serving as a counselor. The healing touch of the empath is a recurring character in mystical fiction. The 1950's tales of The People by Zenna Henderson tells of a gifted empathic race who settled in rural Arizona. A search on the internet may link you to angels, healers, and sensitives — all evoking the word empath. Most empaths are not psychic or paranormal in spectacular ways, but the intensity of their receptivity is apparent.

Sensitive, caring, responsive people - these are the empaths. Their language reflects their inner experience. You will hear them say that they sense things, "feel into" things, are moved by things. They experience life in a connected way that is often described as emotional. They flow easily with their feelings. Laughing out loud, crying at a line in a song or at the movement of music itself. Whatever attracts them -- people, animals, art, theatre, music, friendships, groups, fields of studies -- comes to them with intensity and passion. Empaths enter into and inhabit fully the aspects of their life. Their capacities are often shared in the helping professions, in the arts, in simply their intimate way of being present with others. You have met them and are moved by them. You are one of them and recognize yourself in this description. It is easy to see the beauty and delight that living with sensitivity can bring. It is clear that others can benefit from the caring responsiveness of an empath. Yet, being an empath is usually a challenging road to walk in life.

Current cognitive science views the capacity for empathy as part of the brain's neural circuitry. We seem to learn to control our actions through a mirroring neuron system that appears to become attuned through personal experience, based on seeing others doing similar actions. Another circuit links this system to the emotion centers of the brain and the physical expression of emotion in the muscles of the face and body. It is felt that together these systems lead to a *capacity* for empathy. Further, it seems that this capacity must be supported and developed or it diminishes. Empath energy brings still another element to this physical root -- inherent qualities that amplify and expand empathy.

You are invited to consider the idea of empath energy in its broadest context. From there we'll examine core principles and aspects of empath nature. Specific concepts and understandings, suggestions, approaches and tools will be explored, especially through the questions and comments shared by individuals who have personally explored empath energy, placing some of what has been discovered in the context of a spiritual psychology to understand ourselves better. Dancers Between Realms is compiled and edited from many years of personal sessions and workshops led by Elisabeth Fitzhugh and the Orion group, focusing on the idea of people living with and often, coping with, the intensive experience of connection with others that is empath energy -- a connection which is *beyond empathy.*

One of life's challenges is that understanding and insight
are part of a kind of 'gathering process' of awareness.
Thus, learning is not as conscious as it might seem.

Many of the choices we make or seem to have made, may not
make sense at first or the sense within them is not clear.

When life is unclear, consider that clarity is simply not yet
available and further, may not become available.

Therefore, the "why's" of life can often
only be explored to a degree.
The "how to be" with life is always available to us.

CHAPTER ONE

UNDERSTANDING YOURSELF AS AN EMPATH

Empaths carry the energy of receptivity
in the essence of their being.
They hold all arenas of receptivity
in a deeply intensive and interwoven way.

Consider empath energy as the capacity to experience connection far beyond the rapport of empathy. We all carry a capacity for empathy. We can be receptive, sensitive and intuitive in varying degrees. Empaths find these qualities amplified in an innate way. They are led by a strong recognition of the energy that flows between people. Energy, in these terms, is the core dynamic quality of life, imbued with capacity for action. It is the current of life that flows through all of us and all things; a *vitality* that can ebb and flow. Energy is experienced as feelings and emotions – your own and others. Energy represents connection – within yourself, between people, with cultures and places. Energy vibrates as a sense of affinity and resonance. Energy is experienced in the physical body, in the realms of the mind and in what is called the heart. Whatever words are used to describe or point toward it, energy is always felt and recognized. The vocabulary and concepts of energy are continually evolving and becoming. In the broadest way, energy *exists*, is present and will make itself known.

Empath energy and awareness is embedded in a broad spiritual perspective that is rooted in the spiritual perspective of the interconnection of all things. As you explore empath energy, you can also recognize a deeper, innate connection to the All, the vast consciousness of being. Bringing a spiritual perspective to your inner work allows awareness through more than your conscious mind.

Empaths experience empathy, sensitivity and intuition in a strongly amplified or even accelerated manner.

Empaths feel very *permeable* to sensing other people and their energy, especially in large groups or crowds and new situations. In addition, this sensitivity also results in an amplification of one's *own* energy. Thus, worries and concerns, reactions and responses can be heightened and feel overwhelming or even invasive. Empaths often do not recognize how the degree of their sensitivity is different from others. Individuals often struggle for a long time before they are able to recognize that they are more receptive and responsive than others they know. Typically, someone else declares, "You're *too* sensitive. You're *too* reactive. You're *too* emotional. *You are too…*" This is often the first time people begin to understand that perhaps they *are* sensitive in a different way. Thus, your first awareness of yourself as an empath comes as a critique and criticism. If you are acculturated as most, this difference is negatively internalized and becomes an effective superego, one you agree with by saying, "I am too sensitive. I am too emotional. I am too much." Many people experience difficulty living with this capacity in this world of immense interaction and input. At the same time you hold qualities of connection that can touch others, building bridges of understanding and compassion.

The customary model of being receptive is reflected in this language of "too much"; implying that one degree of emotion or sensitivity is acceptable, but other degrees of response are *not*. Sensitivity is seen only as a byproduct of psychological development or the conditioning of life experience. Empath sensitivity is an innate quality, neither optional nor a mental choice. The empath system of receptivity and sensitivity is intensely acute; an integral part of the mental, emotional and physical self. Consider this receptivity as "empath DNA." The term highlights that this quality is innate, intertwined and embedded, not something you can just get over, throw out or deny. When you consider your sensitivity as part of your *physicality*, you open to a different perspective.

> Empath nature expands like a sponge;
> absorbing into itself all the fluid energy,
> contact and content of interaction with others.

The difficulty with such a receptive capacity is that there is often confusion about what is in the original "sponge" and that which is filling it. "Do I feel this way within myself or have I absorbed this from another?" A further challenge is that most empaths are not aware of the intensity or fullness of their receptive nature until certain events occur that feel interfering or even dangerous to the self. You find yourself saying, "I did not feel like myself," or others say, "You are not acting like yourself," etc. Hints come into the conscious mind that something *other* than the self is interacting in their lives.

> It is vital for empaths to consciously
> explore, understand and address
> the energetic flow in their lives.

You begin to learn about empath energy by first *recognizing* it as a principle – empathy energy is an innate capacity for deeply intensive receptivity. From there, you can begin to consciously address and question your receptivity, responsiveness and the actions which flow from them. Naturally, this amplified receptivity impacts one's psycho-social-emotional development. Simple inquiry will lead you to learn your own patterns and eventually bring your attention to working with and managing the flow of input. Begin by wondering, "Does this idea of empath nature speak to me? Do I sense myself in these descriptions?" This may lead to asking, "When is this my energy alone? When am I receiving or responding as an empath?" You can ask, "If I am receiving in this empath mode and if this feeling is *not* mine, what am I to do with it? Can I have clarity as to what this energy is?" Listen to what arises from such questions and allow yourself to discover and apply what you sense.

Begin to recognize yourself as an empath by exploring your interactions in daily life.

Following are situations empaths experience and are often challenged by. Note which of these you resonate with, recognize or respond to.

Empaths deeply feel and respond to the environment. Big crowds are difficult. Bars and parties are very challenging, especially the social cocktail party. It is as if a very loud and strong flow of energy is pouring into you. Often one glass of beer or wine helps soften your receptivity. But by the second, alcohol seems to amplify your sensitivity and everything is even more heightened. Empaths *feel* other people. They know someone is upset. They know when someone has a headache. They know something is going on with this one or that one, even if they can't tell what it is. Empaths go out and have a lovely time and the next morning they feel sick, a little flu-ish, a headache perhaps. They wonder if it was what they ate or someone's perfume. The assumed cause of sensitivity seems to vary – one time it's this food, another time not. They start to think they are chemically sensitive. "Maybe I've got allergies or gluten intolerance or changing hormones." The specifics change all the time. Empaths feel sensitive to everything and the body will learn to respond to this sensitivity. Sensitivity seems to grow more as you get older or lose weight or from other changes in the body or environment.

After a while empaths have no energy. At these times, they want to just stay in and not answer the phone or check e-mail. They can't even watch television or a movie or read a book. They want to rest and take a nap. They want to lie in a hot bath and put a herbal pillow over their eyes. They want to go for a walk in the park alone. They can't take the Metro or bus one more time, yet driving is worse! As too much input intensifies, empaths start to feel depressed. They think they *are* depressed.   Actually they are energetically exhausted.   All these examples lead to one conclusion: recognizing you are a hyper-sensitive person.   That recognition can then expand into further understanding of how, why and what contributes to that sensitivity.

Build understanding of yourself with self-inquiry.

As you begin to more fully recognize the nature of yourself, you add to your own empirical history of awareness question by question, observation by observation and insight by insight.   Ask yourself, "What if I really am a hyper-sensitive person? What if I am so permeable that I pick up all these energies? How do I consider this? How do I manage it?"   And most importantly of all, "How do I understand and interpret it?"   This history of awareness creates a lasting foundation of reference on which to base future considerations. But remember, do not solidify your understanding into fixed ideas that are not open to change and further insight.   There is a gap between what we come to know and what we do. Awareness tries to bridge this gap, but can only do so when fluidity is included in your understanding.

It is difficult to be conscious of that which feels innate. Picture empath nature as an emotional-biophysical energy system of strong receptivity.

Most people are not consciously aware of their innate processes. You don't hear every heartbeat or feel your blood flow and in a way, empath nature is like that. It is not only an emotional sensitivity. Empath nature is an emotional-biophysical energy field: a complex, interconnected system of strong receptivity operating in the background, like your physical autonomic processes. The image of empath DNA or genes is a useful model to see the system as innate. The more aware you are that there can be such a system, the more you have the conscious option to manage your responses. You can more readily apply ideas and concepts and make use of tools and techniques.

Recognizing your empath nature begins with allowing that at your core you are receptive and sensitive. Rather than identifying yourself as special, be willing take responsibility toward this nature of your being. "My receptivity feels beyond empathy and intuition. I need to recognize concepts and strategies to support me in this understanding and be responsible to it." Recognizing one's capacity to *receive* seems readily available. Managing and moving *with* this receptivity typically requires more conscious attention. Once you are more in touch with seeing yourself as an empath, you can become more in touch with the actual attitudes, techniques and tools that facilitate *being* an empath. You might then ask, "How else can I work with this? Can I share it with intent? Can I serve and support another with my empath nature?"

Along with a sense of "empath DNA" for intense receptivity,
many people also carry a feeling of Otherness.

Empaths often express that they feel different from or "other" than most people; too sensitive and affected by things. Some people experience this intensely, even feeling they are different than this reality. Still others have shared their sense that there is a "somewhere else" where empath energy is customary and understood. The idea arises that there is an empath milieu of receptivity and sensitivity; an empath culture. Many people report visuals of such otherwheres. They share images of other places and groups. As one man put it, "I am one of a group and we are empathetic together. We are feeling *together* in a way that is unlike anything I know." Such images allow you to recognize and resonate, i.e., understand and match the vibration, with qualities regarded as different. Since these elements may not be directly reflected in your present life, you can connect with the *principle* of the qualities as seen in another place, time or culture. You may also connect with the *energies* of these times and places, but more often, such images are your *interpretations* of what you sense, based on your present knowledge. The principle within the images is what will consistently serve you.

Consider that there *are* realms of being, realms of consciousness that one can connect to and resonate with. Consider that there were and are societies of empaths. The core principle of such a society would be that cultural customs and practices would evolve out of empath nature and support living with intense receptivity. In such a society, empath capacities would be seen as innate and individuals would be taught how to work with their receptivity. The culture would understand how energy can be modulated and transformed. Presently, the ability to recognize and change energy is often *not* readily understood or considered an innate trait. It is useful to consider this possibility as you develop your own inner models.

> **Embedded within your empath receptivity is an equal capacity to manage and work with the energy you receive.**

The sensitive and receptive quality of empath nature is more readily recognized by yourself and others. The capacity to understand and work with your receptivity may feel less available or even dormant, but it is present, another thread of the empath DNA. There are three main aspects to managing energy – a triad of translation, transmutation and transducing. Translating is readily finding another way to convey meaning or comprehension. Transmutation allows the energy received to simply move through you and change. Transducing modulates, softens and steps-down energy. When you use these capacities you are not *directing* change, declaring "Make this bad energy good." The individual mind does not need to direct the universe, nor can it do so. You can use your mind as a focus of conscious intent, serving as a *channel* for energy. You can at times *direct* energy, but it is essential that you be centered in your willingness to *release the outcome* and your own image of what that outcome would look like. Knowing you are part of the All, you can allow energy received to pass through you and be shifted by the vastness and not your own egoic ideas. In your deeper connection to the All, you can gather awareness and knowledge through *recognition,* a quality that is a deep knowing fuller than conscious learning and includes resonance and sensing.

9

Abilities of the empath are reflected in how individuals interact with people psychologically and emotionally.

Empaths are drawn to professions and careers that reflect their essence as people who can readily absorb and change energy: the triad of translating, transmuting and transducing. Empaths may serve as *translators* -- literally and qualitatively. In the workplace, you may take one set of information and make a translation for another group. You try to help those in different situations find the same language, to come to an understanding -- mediators, managers, counselors. Empaths facilitate *transmutation*, changing energy as in helping others to let go of one feeling and allowing another. They can also *transduce* energy, softening intense feelings by finding another way of speaking or sharing a principle in more subtle ways.

Empaths often study philosophy, psychology and explore spirituality to find and experience connection. They are drawn to developing a broad perspective as a way to feel part of the world. Other empaths find expression and connection through a focus on the Arts. Robert DeNiro or Johnny Depp are actors who *become* their characters. They absorb the identity of the character and merge their own awareness with it until they become expressions of the essence of the character. When a project ends, they release and *transmute* the energy of the characters they have inhabited. In other arenas, such as poetry, painting and music, empaths merge with the energy they receive or sense and their art is *itself* the transmutation of the energy.

Empaths hold the ability to touch into and absorb knowledge and awareness in many ways, not only in response to emotions. Many of the images of shamans, magicians and healers in other ages reflect qualities of the empath. The model of the shaman also reflects those who come into *conscious* recognition of their nature -- working with their abilities with thoughtfulness and awareness, and most often, from an attitude of service to others. The model of responsibility and service is important to consider and embrace.

> The biggest mistake empaths make
> is misinterpreting what one senses.

Not only can empaths misinterpret what they receive from others, they often make incorrect assessments about themselves. How easily you can say, "If I have no energy, I must be depressed." How quickly one can decide, "If my body is sensitive, it can only mean I'm allergic to this or that." Empaths first learn to recognize that they *do* sense energy and feelings from others. But *sensing* feelings does not innately mean you accurately understand the meaning. Problems arise not from the fact that you sensed something, but from your interpretation. Misinterpretation is a core challenge for empaths. It impacts your sense of your inner world and how you respond to the outer world and is a main source of problems in interpersonal relating.

> Images of empath nature abound in myth,
> folktales, mystical fiction and film.

A prominent image of the empath is in an episode of Star Trek © [1968, episode 63, The Empath] in which we see a young woman who can touch another and literally take onto herself their pain or wound and transform and heal it. This is probably the most consistent and persistent image of the empath; an expression of empath consciousness that continues to resonate strongly. You can learn more from this image because the empath has become afraid of her receptivity. She is alone and isolated from her culture and there is no one to teach her how to manage the energy she receives. As she eventually learns, along with the empaths' amplification of receptivity there is also amplification of one's capacity to manage the effects of the receptivity. As you become aware of and understand how your empath systems work, you will also recognize more deeply your own innate capabilities to work with what you receive. You may not literally absorb wounds as our science fiction empath does, but you will still find it essential to understand and learn how to balance your receptivity and the actions that flow from it.

"Empath nature" is a useful model of your receptivity.
Yet, do not create or amplify an identity as an empath.

Thinking of empath nature as a model of being helps objectify your experiences and places them in a context. The term "model" refers to a *flexible* and *changeable* form of understanding and conceptualization. It is not the purpose of this model to create or amplify your *identity* as an empath. When identities become fixed and ideas of the self are *unconscious,* there is a great capacity for that identity to actually *interfere* with growth and development. An unconscious identity is no longer questioned or examined and is not open to shift and change. Solidifying an inner picture of yourself as an empath risks limiting fuller exploration of the very qualities you want to explore. Use the empath model as a framework and a conceptual tool. At times it may feel your empath qualities are totally the innate nature of your being. This sense can be useful because it identifies your feelings, as in, "This is how I feel. I am this receptive being some call empath." This identification is a crystallizing experience; a moment on which you can build awareness and recognition of your nature. Yet, do *not* attach, bind, or solidify such moments. Doing so is like putting yourself in a box and labeling it "empath." Unquestioned identification can readily become a limitation. When you label and box yourself, you close the door to growth. There is no expansion, because in holding to your identity, you are essentially declaring, "I can't grow further because I know *all* there is to know about my empath nature."

Allow your awareness to support you in discovering yourself.

There is great value in "freeing-up" conceptualizations. Make use of conceptualizations and at the same time, be willing to let them shift, change and grow. Allow and *invite* yourself to see differently what you saw or understood before. You cannot do this if you do not allow the changing or perhaps even the *undoing,* of what you have known. The letting go of the known can be scary, difficult and challenging. It is also the most invigorating, vitality-filled way to live. This willingness to let go, explore and discover can take you for a life's journey all the way through the very last passage. You can come into death with awareness and curiosity, perhaps asking as you enter this singular journey, "What else can I see? What can I now know?" You are making it up as you go along, without clear blueprints and maps.

Empath energy opens the door to depths of responsiveness and understanding. Your personal self-discovery contributes to the further understanding of an evolving consciousness of connection.

As you come to understand yourself as an empath, consider that there are techniques and tools to support you in your sensitivity and capacities.

Consider that you *can* manage your response to the energy. Consider that you may have this sensitive empath quality, but do not need to be buffeted by it or be led to inaccurate understandings of your nature. Come to understand your nature in a more *neutral* way. By objectifying your experiences and making them an object of your inquiry and understanding, you give yourself a place to stand as an observer or witness of yourself. This observer position is deeply supportive to seeing yourself and your situations clearly.

As your perspective broadens and deepens, you will more fully see and comprehend your own motivations and actions, and recognize how energy comes to you. You can access inner knowledge of empath nature. You will find mechanisms, devices and structures that will support you in personal growth and life. Focus your attention on understanding and integrating the principles of empath energy. By placing attention on the principle, specifics and details of approaches and techniques will emerge from *each* situation. Understanding the principle also establishes an awareness that *alerts* you to be conscious of your situations and choices. For example, once you anchor the principle that you can choose to be open or closed to receptivity, you will more readily become aware of when you are being inundated by receptivity. You can then analyze the sensed energy and ask, "Is this energy I need to receive or is this the energy of those people over there?" Pausing to question leads to clear understanding. When understanding is clear, there is usually no quandary. When your actions are not clear to yourself, that is *exactly* the time to question.

Empaths' innate and natural abilities
carry with them the responsibility of *balance.*

It is also your responsibility to hold a balanced view of your capacities and abilities. Do not exalt these innate capacities or give them excessive authority. Do not be seduced by the idea that because you *can* change or transmute energy, it is your cosmic mandate *to* transmute energy. Your empath capacities are primarily for your own benefit and carry the responsibility of thoughtfulness and humbleness, especially should you offer your sensings or help to others. Balance and discernment are supported when you are willing to consider that your mind and its wants and desires are not the only perspective to ponder. A spiritual perspective can serve as a tool of balance. Considering that there is awareness more expansive than yourself, you can take a moment to check your ideas and decisions with the grand Web of Interconnection, the Vastness, the All or whatever term you use to signify that which is fuller than the egoic personality. Simply ask, "Do I see this clearly? Is it time for action?" Be willing and comfortable to consider what responses come to you, including letting a situation go or releasing the energy without interaction. The power of *balance*, of learning when to work with energy or when to simply close or release, supports your foundation for conscious life as an empath. Developing this balancing may lead you to discover ways to apply and make clear use of your abilities.

Learning to balance and manage receptivity is essential.

Empaths express themselves with vocabulary that reflects their receptivity. You talk of "getting it," sensing "something's going on" and "picking up" what was felt or said. All these terms can be seen as the unconscious revealing to you the nature of your being. But most importantly, having the *ability* to absorb energy does not mean you are supposed to absorb anything and everything. It is your right and responsibility to balance your receptivity with discernment and boundaries. Learning to balance and manage your receptivity is essential. A first step to this balance is to create a personal symbolic system that signifies to yourself that you are either open or closed. The simplest tool is saying, "I am open to receive" or "I am closed at this time." You may qualify your statement, as in, "I am closed to this energy, but I am willing to hear the information. I am closed to the energy at this time, but willing to receive it at another time."

Developing such discernment and setting boundaries are aspects of your personal inner work. Self-inquiry is the essential tool to understanding all that moves, motivates and colors your view of the world. Inquiry, though, does not *guarantee* resolution and solution. As you grow in your understanding of what impacts, moves and motivates you, you will discover many tools you already use subconsciously. You will soon find that using such tools consistently and with conscious attention supports ease and balance in life and the capacity to be *with* whatever arises just as it is.

Images come to awareness that help you comprehend reality.

People receive images and associations in dreams, while musing or without a prompt. Usually the image can be placed in a cultural or historical context. As with the reports of empath groups and other places, what is most important is not the literal image, but the principle you see *within* the image. When such images arise there is a central *quality* connecting and resonating with you. Examining these qualities can be useful. There is often some congruency to the information within the image and your present situation. If you were to see yourself as a clockmaker in 18th century Germany, you can see within the image *qualities* of precision and order. Would you be supported by precision and order? Do you judge your need for precision and order? Use your *associations* to the images as a prompt for inquiry. Again, do not make these associations and understandings into fixed identities that will box you into a singular understanding.

A conceptual model is not necessarily the truth –
it is a tool that uses language to point *toward* the truth.

Using the clockmaker image, one could say, "I feel this connection with myself as a clockmaker and see how it reflects my attraction to detail." This is how one *says* it. This is how you can *talk* about and understand it, but what you have actually done is *resonate* with the image. When you take such resonances and images and place them into conceptual terms, you are limited by *language* and what you already understand. Remember you do not have the full picture; you may not even have *access* to the whole picture. In fact, you may not have any way to even comprehend the whole truth. Look at history and you will see again and again how people understood something in one way and now it is understood differently. It is very challenging to completely break out of your own cultural constructs and understand something not of or other than your own world. The balance point is in simply allowing that your understanding may not be the whole truth.

As you bring your attention to your life, you will find your *own* energetic system begins to create patterns that support you. The idea is *not* to create rules or unconnected external structures. By paying attention to what you are already doing, and to do it with more attention, you can consciously *support* the nature of your being. If you have diabetes, you have to learn how to eat differently so that your condition doesn't flare and bother you. The metaphor is the same. "If I understand the nature of my being more, I can then find patterns and tools that support me." Again, the essential tool of awareness is self-inquiry and the willingness you bring to it. The focus is to let your attention be attuned to what is going on with you and what you need *now*. You'll find you will have tools available; tools anchored in principle as supportive structures

Your personal exploration of empath energy contributes to an evolving gestalt of awareness.

Empath awareness is an example of the "100th monkey" principle. In this, individual members of a group experience, explore and discover new ideas or approaches.   One by one, the energy of this new awareness comes together until at a point when the "100th monkey" -- the 100th person in the group -- has experienced the new idea, the vibration of the idea reaches a critical mass of energy. This mass of connected energy creates a *gestalt* - a wholeness of knowing that incorporates more than the sum of the individual parts. The gestalt knowing then translates into a paradigm shift, a shift of awareness, that can extend beyond the initial group and energetically become available to and recognized by others. This change occurs around the world as an energetic flow of communication, without direct contact. As you personally discover and explore more deeply your empath nature, you are contributing to the building of a gestalt recognizing the essence of the empath connection and way of operating.

> Empaths are Dancers Between Realms –
> carrying a quiet song of receptivity and responsiveness
> in a world that can be loud, harsh and insensitive.

Aware empaths continually attempt to recognize two different systems of being. They choose to recognize how they operate and have evolved on one level, while learning and participating in another. What is before you is to create your own integral expression of Wholeness and express it in the everyday facets of living - work, relationships and events -- all the ups and downs of life. Holding this kind of conscious attention is really quite extraordinary. Acknowledge and honor the energy you are giving to your aware life. Allow yourself to also experience the deep joy and satisfaction of living as true to yourself as you can.

Activate your inner knowledge and awareness of your nature.
Allow these core aspects of empath nature to become
integral parts of how you consider yourself.

- Empaths have an innate strong field of receptivity and responsiveness.

- Empaths carry a capacity to manage the energy they receive; to translate, transmute and transduce.

- By consciously learning more about your own nature, its sensitivity and requirements, you can find ways to experience your capacities with more harmony and balance.

- Accept the responsibility that empath nature requires balance and discernment.

- Adopt self-inquiry as a primary tool of awareness.

- Be conscious of the difficulties that can arise from misinterpretation of what you sense and the egoic direction of your intent and energy.

- Consider that there can be purpose and meaning in your different energy; that by simply living your life you are bringing new energy into further recognition.

- Continue to discover and learn more about yourself and the nature of your empath essence.

In further chapters, these principles and tools will be explored in more detail, especially through questions and comments shared by people like you -- participants in workshops and personal sessions exploring their own empath nature.

CHAPTER TWO

TOOLS AND TECHNIQUES OF AWARENESS

The principle of these tools and techniques is to
reactivate what empaths *innately* know.
Transmuting. Transducing. Managing energy.

Consider that you *can* manage your response to energy. Consider that you may have a quality in the nature of your being that amplifies your sensitivity. Rather than be buffeted by this quality, rather than have your sensitivity lead to false understanding of your nature, you can come to an understanding that is neutral. This neutral consideration provides a solid, stronger base to stand on as you look within yourself.

Again, empath nature is a field of strong receptivity operating all the time; an autonomic emotional-biophysical energy system. As it is difficult to be conscious of something that feels *innate*, use the image of Empath DNA or genes to hold this principle that supports conscious action, using images or ideas to *manage* your receptivity and the energy received. A primary focus for empaths is finding ways to manage being overwhelmed by too much input and learning to *transduce*, i.e., step down the energy It is very useful for empaths to have concrete, solid symbols to represent moving energy. When you feel too much input, touching something actual, like a crystal or rock, can serve as a reminder that you need to lessen the input. Looking at an image, like a picture of the ocean or mountains or hearing a sound, as in certain music, can serve in the same way.

Choose objects that are meaningful to you as symbols of balance, grounding, renewal, etc. Begin by finding a symbol that represents modulating energy. Ask within, "What holds the idea of stepping down energy?" See what image arises. See what you discover already in your environment. That lovely rock you found in the park may be just the right thing. The idea that the rock represents balance merges with the actuality of the rock and your "symbol" emerges. Add to this a pattern or ritual that also holds the idea that you are choosing to modulate energy and rebalance. It can be as simple as "I will make a cup of tea. Hold my rock. Look at my picture of the ocean. And take a deep breath." All of these things work together to bring concrete focus to your attention and intention. They emphasize that you have the right and responsibility to *initiate* changing how you feel and respond. Symbols and routines amplify your intention. The solidness of the rock amplifies grounding. The ocean amplifies mutability through ebb and flow. The ever-symbolic cup of tea represents taking a moment to care for yourself.   These simple acts are easy to incorporate into daily life on a consistent basis and are actually powerful tools of balance.

It would seem possible that once you've established such a balancing, transducing routine it would flow all the time. Like most aspects of life, your focus can easily become unconscious and you will find yourself overwhelmed by input once again. The brain itself designed to place knowledge in the background, to make it subconscious and therefore automatic, that is useful and effective. It is challenging, though, when you are trying to learn new approaches or change patterns. Rather than be frustrated with this trait, simply acknowledge it. You cannot create a one-time "fix." Instead you are observing and learning what occurs for you and gathering strategies to use as situations arise. You are creating a tool box of ideas, principles and items that remind you to *question* and move toward balance. You set these tools in motion with your conscious intent; training yourself by applying the tools concretely or consistently for a time. The tools serve as support in bringing conscious attention to each situation. If you feel overwhelmed at work, you activate several tools by simply stating, "Maybe I should make sure I take more breaks at work, hang a picture of the ocean in my cubicle and clear my head by walking home from the office." You acknowledge that you are responding to input. You remember that you can consciously affect that response. You recall some of the symbols of balance and see that you can rebalance in many ways, from taking a break to walking home.

Tools amplify the focus of your intention.
Tools help you discern your own degrees of receptivity.

In addition to concrete symbols, you can use a symbolic *energetic* tool to modulate energy by creating a symbol and invoking it when you know you are going into a challenging situation. Many people use the image of a spiral of energy as a symbol of transmutation as it evokes movement. As you hold the intent of transmuting, transforming, transducing or filtering energy, you can clearly picture how energy

e spiral and follow the spiral up or down to change
gy. Begin with the spiral image and see what
o you. The spiral image is often reported as being
filled with a moving light. Others share seeing the spiral as the dark
blue of night sky, expressing their connection to deep space. Deep
purple and shades of iridescent green are other images shared. Your
experience may echo these examples. The idea is to discover what
image arises from your own sense of filtering or transformation.

Direct awareness of your experiences leads to creating effective tools
of support. Link the idea of a spiral to a moment when you are really
experiencing and recognizing your response. "I am overwhelmed and
need to rebalance." Distill that feeling into the image, such as the
spiral or into a key-word representing the action needed, as in
"rebalance." You can combine the spiral image with the keyword
rebalance. Eventually the key-word can literally activate an energetic
process of rebalancing and becomes a tool you initiate consciously.
As you see more clearly the situations that overwhelm you, you can
use your rebalancing symbol to set a filter in place before you become
overwhelmed. The tool is now both responsive and proactive. Using
your tools consistently aligns them with you more innately and renders
them more effective.

In this language of images, it is important to remember that tools may
arise which are not *visual* images. They may be *sounds* like singing or
toning. They may occur as *actions* such as movement or breathing or
involve touch, texture, scent and taste. All these variations serve to

remind us of why we have to listen within and discover our ᴄ
variations of the tools and techniques.

Linking intention and attention
with symbols and icons
amplifies the energy.

Linking something *physical* along with an image or intent solidifies
the energy. Snap your fingers or touch your fingers together as you
picture the spiral of rebalance. If you wear jewelry, touch your ring,
pendant or bracelet. Linking the word with physical reality amplifies
and grounds the energy of your intent. You can also say the word out
loud, adding the physical aspect of hearing the sound as well as feeling
the vibration of your vocal chords. All of this builds the energy very
solidly and it makes it more and more effective.

As you begin creating tools, work with each step consciously.

- Hold your intent and picture the image.
- Say the word or phrase.
- Touch and anchor to an object, like a rock or jewelry.
- Touch and anchor with your body, as in touching the fingers
  together.

Recognize which aspect -- the image, word, or touch -- seems to
crystallize the whole process for you. As you literally learn and

Awareness

Awareness

ʋıı

echnique, you will find that using the crystallized
ing your ring, will essentially activate the process.

There are many traditions of linking physical reality with energetic principles. Symbolic energy is linked to and anchored within the physical actions in the rituals of religious and spiritual practices. Rituals construct a form that invites and allows the energy to flow through. There is a similar focus in ancient traditions as in honoring the winds, the directions, the nature elements - fire, water, air. Life is energy in physical form. You are energy in physical form. Allow yourself to become a channel for vitality, balance and change.

After a time, you might find a tool seems less effective as your awareness and intent becomes more unconscious. When this occurs, simply return to doing the complete process, essentially rebuilding your technique. Specifically including the physical touching is usually the most effective, as it supports translating *energetic* reality, which has a different intensity and velocity, into the density and pace of *physical* reality. Techniques create a focus of attention that helps you discern your degree of receptivity and interaction with others. They can help you manage being in the world without being buffeted, overwhelmed, drained or exhausted.

The idea of Cloaking is to find an image
that allows you to feel open and permeable
to a degree that is comfortable and useful.

"Cloaking" is a most useful technique. The principle is again based on recognizing heightened receptivity. "What can I do about that receptivity?" Most of you already have your own ways; withdrawal is the primary choice reported. Some people withdraw and follow up with aggression to keep the energy away, presenting a grumpy curmudgeon front. Others use withdrawal and depression, presenting a sad, exhausted face that says, "Oh, I can't do it any more," and all variations in-between. When you become more conscious of the idea of heightened receptivity, you are aware that "This is a taxing situation for me." Rather than just reverting to personality defenses you have already established, you can become conscious of your capacity to *manage* the input of receptivity. This is where you can transmute, transduce and literally cloak yourself with energy.

The intent is literally embedded in saying, "I have this very sensitive receptivity. I am going to build an energetic cloak around me. I am going to go into the situation thinking I really want to be open to connection, but I don't want to be all unfiltered and permeable." One is not building a wall; one is building a kind of filter. You are not guarding; you are simply *filtering*. When you *neutrally* consider the empath genetic receptivity, then techniques of managing input and response do not have to be defensive. You can have space, you can have a filter; you can have a boundary. You can limit easily and comfortably, not in a psychologically defensive, emotional way. You speak for yourself clearly but gently, when you say, "I'm a sensitive person. Please don't do that. Stop now."

One person actually had a cloak made. He had a particular image that became a quite beautiful blue velvet cape, lined with a silken fabric of stars. The cloaking symbol which came to him was that he was surrounded by stars. This image allowed the flow of energy to be comforting and transmuting. He wore his magical cloak only privately at home, but carried the image with him as his symbol of the energy of cloaking and filtering.

Another person used the image of a waterfall; picturing the waterfall flowing in front of him, filtering the energy. Many people use the webs or spirals of energy imagery. The image of a balloon of energy surrounding you is also useful. One woman found she could mentally understand being permeable and allowing energy to flow through, but none of the images shared by other people really worked for her. She discovered that her round net bath sponge matched exactly her image of energy flowing through. She even has carried it with her as a concrete symbol of permeability. Another person uses a similar sponge image to release her own emotions. At times she actually squeezes water out of a sponge to amplify her intent of letting emotions flow through and transmute. Discover what allows *you* to be open and permeable to a degree that is comfortable and effective.

**There is a consistent need for empaths
to create Renewal Zones –
actions and situations that
renew energy and well-being.**

Many empaths experience emotional and energetic exhaustion which is typically perceived as depression. Life is an ebb and flow and simply, when you have too much flow in or out, you become *ebbed*. You become fallow and drained. The culture teaches you to ignore your own ebb and flow, even Nature's ebb and flow. You are asked to be active 24/7, to just push on through, to "just do it." Illness and depression are two of the few permitted places to ebb. There is not much language for "I am in a low energy state," which is of course, a most natural event. Sleep is an *ebb* and a daily requirement for the body. Why would there not be other kinds of ebbs in daily life?

If you look at your life and you see that you always have to "crash" on Friday night – guess what? You do! Bring your attention to that need, that pattern and *ritualize* it. Make it really special. "You know I really do need Friday nights off." Let yourself declare that Friday is not a night to go out. It's a night to go home, not answer the phone or check email. It's a time to relax and be off duty. The more you anchor these *attention zones*, in which you pay attention to what you need and do, the more they will work *for* you and *support* you. And in that you are creating your own *renewal zones* – actions and situations that renew your energy and well-being.

> As you bring attention to your life, you will find your own
> energetic system begins to create patterns that support you.

Bring your attention towards discovering your own patterns. Look into your life, feel into it and ask, "Where is my ebb place?" Simple inquiry will readily reveal your own patterns because you *do* know them, even if you do not always allow them. Is it always Saturday morning you like to sleep in? Is Sunday your day off? Find the one that is *true.* Is it every two weeks, not once a week? Individuals who look within and listen to themselves build on awareness and create their own energetic retreats and havens. They establish their own patterns of renewal. These patterns are then available and waiting for you to access them. Sometimes if you really need to do something that is very stressful, you can make it through till Friday night – because Friday is always there as your *renewal night.* Your energetic system will begin to create patterns that support you. Again, you are bringing your attention to what you need and how it can best work for you. The idea is not to create rules or external structures, but to become aware of what you are already doing to bring in a more *conscious attention* to support the nature of your being.

We readily shift our approaches to manage various health conditions. The metaphor applies in the idea that the more you understand your nature, the more you can find patterns and tools that support you. If you apply some of these tools, you will feel the difference. When you forget about it, "Oh, I'm not doing that this week," after awhile you will feel off-balance or overwhelmed. All you will need to do is remember, "Oh yes, I need to take Friday nights for myself again."

Be interested in the "long haul" – awareness for the fullness of your life, not only the present or the peaks or aha's. Use the tool box concept of principles and approaches as they are needed, rather than techniques which must be done every Wednesday at 8:00 AM. The real task is to let your attention be *attuned* to inquiring into what is going on with you and what you need *now*. You'll have tools available, not a rigid structure. Your tool box should not be seen as armor or a shield; a heavy bag you carry with you ready to cope with every difficulty. Rather, think of it as a backpack. It's there, ready to be opened, but it's not the focus of attention. You are walking open to the world, knowing you have support available.

> Because empaths are *merged* in a hyper-receptivity,
> they don't know it *is* hyper or expanded receptivity.
> That very differentiation has to be learned.

In a personal session, a client shared, "I can control a lot of aspects of my life, but there is this one compartment I cannot control – my own mind. Specifically, I cannot control my obsessive thinking and worrying and anger about the attitudes and frictions I have at the job. It's so bad that it is like a switch I cannot turn off. The only thing I have found that can stop it is deep meditation, which I don't always have the chance to do. Even if I promise myself and goad myself by saying, "I am going to stop. I am going to have a positive attitude. I'm going to vibrate more positively and therefore attract more positive experiences." In an instant I have forgotten that I have made that assertion and I'm back in my mind with angry statements and thoughts. There is nothing wrong, per se, with anger but this has become completely taxing."

31

This is an excellent experiential example of the *untransmuted* empath. The body-mind system is very workman-like. It will find the most direct and least sophisticated approach to deal with stress. If someone has an injury and part of the body becomes weak, that place will be where stress shows up in the future. It is not that the part is weak per se, but that it has become more *permeable*. It is an opening for energy to flow through. So the mind, in this case, is trying to fight and push off the energy that is being held within the *empathic nervous system*. It is as if the "personality nervous system" has an overlay or additional aura, i.e., the "empathic nervous system."

> Empath nature is the lens you
> see and experience through.

The great bane of the empath is as they are so merged in their own experience, it takes consistent awareness to recall that this additional nervous system is present and influential. Remember to step back and say a version of *"Am I in receptive mode? Am I receiving much more than I have any awareness of?"* If you have hypersensitive hearing, this is simply how your hearing operates. Your true option is to remember you are sensitive to the input around you and discover how to modulate what you receive because you are not able to modify every environment. You learn the pitches and tones that affect you. You learn the situations to avoid or places to wear ear-plugs. In the dilemma of feeling unable to control one's mind, thoughts feel obsessive because they are actually trying to combat the milieu itself -- in this case, your workplace.

The persistent feeling of being overwhelmed by your thoughts and attitudes is brought about by the mind trying to fend off what it is receiving. You are overwhelmed because you are sensitive to the whole environment. It is as if you are in energetic pollution and are having an allergic reaction. The angry thoughts and feelings are the mind's response to the input. What you have not taken into account is the idea that the environment itself may be a cause of your response, as when unseen pollen causes an allergic reaction. The environment may not be toxic to everyone else; but *you* are hyper-sensitive to it. When you recognize this possibility, you can manage your response by transducing and transmuting -- stepping down your receptivity and releasing what you received.

> The conceptual base of the empath is anchored in
> "My receptivity is amplified. I am permeable and
> sensitive to my energetic environment."

From this principle you can consider clearing or enhancing the environment itself as a way to support and rebalance the situation. You can also see your response in a more neutral, less personal or emotional way. From this neutral place, you have more energy available to find a strategy or solution to a problem, not just a reaction.

Using the allergy metaphor, anger and frustration erupts as if you suddenly broke out in hives, i.e., "I'm allergic to something here. I am getting too much input." It is similar to an allergic reaction which occurs from overloading the system. When you eat something too consistently or in too much quantity, you can bring about a hive response.   In this case, you are overloaded by the conscious and unconscious feelings and emotions you are sensing at work and the mind begins to swirl in reaction. The anger is the "hives" from your *reaction,* not the reality of the situation.

It is not effective to try to just stop the reactive mind-swirl by saying "I am going to control this and create the opposite feeling." When you declare, "I am going to have a positive attitude," your mind essentially responds with, "Are you kidding?! We cannot have a positive attitude -- we're under attack. *We're overwhelmed!"*

**When you feel caught in a mind-swirl of reaction,
the first step is to simply acknowledge
what is occurring just as it is.**

Acknowledge, "I am under stress and having a reaction." Treat the reactive pattern like a friend who is trying to help you, but whose help is not useful in the moment. You would still acknowledge that your friend's *intent* was to help you. When the body reacts to a physical external stimulus, such as an insect bite, you simply accept it and move on from there to cope with the reaction. Here you can begin accepting the situation by saying, "Okay mind, you're reacting. Let's see what really can help here." Feeling overwhelmed by input from your environment is a neutral description of the situation. The anger and obsession are part of the reaction. They are also emotionally laden terms and focusing on them exacerbates your response. Return to the root empath principle that you receive energy. "I am holding energy. I have forgotten that I am permeable to energy and that I need to release it." Once again use the tools that act as a concrete link between your conscious reality and your expanded sensitivity.

In the workplace a version of the cloaking technique is applicable. A filtering image would also be useful. The cloak, waterfall or spiral image would serve. Amplify the image by connecting it with the physical, using an object or touching your fingers together, etc. Do this technique consciously and deliberately. Remember throughout the day and at the end of the day to do something that symbolically acts as a trigger to *transmute* - change and release - any energy you have received. You don't need to pay attention to the specific details of the energy. The problem is that you are sensing feelings that are not connected directly to you. Rather, they are less defined, non-specific experiences which lead to the feeling of being overwhelmed. If a situation is interpersonal or one that needs to be directly addressed, it will be clear to you.

Elements of nature are powerfully beneficial tools of focus and awareness.

Bring nature into your work area to serve as an anchor and a visual tool of attention. Choose something that holds, both visually and tactilely, the energy of rooting and grounding that personally resonates with you. When you resonate with something you recognize and match its vibration, often the quality you are connecting with, as in rootedness, is intensified and enriched. A plant is ideal to anchor nature – a natural crystal or rock; a shell or fossil will serve well. Nature supports allowing the movement of energy and transmutation.

Choose images that evoke your connection to nature. Ancient Redwood trees, a waterfall, the desert or a favorite spot in the nearby park -- whatever speaks to you. Capture an image and frame it; set it as a screensaver or background screen image on your computer.

When worrying, or negative thoughts arise or you feel edgy or concerned, consciously take a meditative break. This can be done subtly and privately in just a moment. Simply take a breath, look at your picture of the sea, hold or touch the stone or shell and set in motion the principle of transmutation. Listen within and discover your own variation.

Empaths often resist using tools and techniques.

Empaths innately, if unconsciously, know how to work with their energy, but this knowledge has not been readily reinforced or mirrored. The resistance to technique seems rooted in a strong memory sense of working with energy in an effortless way as an ordinary part of life. There is unconscious resistance to recognizing that the current environment requires understanding to be at times conscious and consistent.

Consistent does *not* mean *constant*. Again, it is ebb and flow. You can go for long periods of time feeling aligned and moving energy in an effortless manner and then suddenly hit an ebb point where your focused attention is needed. If you adopt the idea that ebb and flow are natural rhythms, you can easily move with them, without judgment or a sense of loss or lack when conscious attention is required.

As you bring transducing and transmuting to the workplace, also become more conscious of *transitioning* after work. Create and use a supportive pattern to shift and transition. Come out of the office and take a breath, visualizing you are breathing out the day's energy. Do a Tai Chi movement or a stretch. Take a brisk walk. Establish one of these small routines as a *signifier* of change and transition. The energy you stepped down at work and transduced will now be transmuted, released and allowed to change on its own.

When you are at home, a shower or bath is still one of the most definite tools of realignment. Remember to specifically hold the idea that you are actually cleansing the *energy system* as you cleanse the body. There are many other cleansing and rebalancing energetic approaches you might discover which can become part of your tool box. When you work from the *principle,* i.e., cleansing the energy system, the principle will open your awareness to all the specifics that are aligned in the present moment.

Music is another strong support to the transducing and transmuting process. See what comes to hand when you look through your music collection with that idea in mind. It may surprise and delight you. Some are moved and balanced by meditative music or deep chanting. Others find opera is the key. Contemporary country or old-time bluegrass releases the energy. Still others find heavy metal, hard rock or hip hop clears the energy best. Notice what else comes to your attention that you can do at work or have in your environment to clear the energy. Discover the indicators that you are becoming sensitive to a situation and find ways to effect the situation before feeling overwhelmed. Ask, "What do I need to do now?" and allow the answer to come present directly or indirectly and without censorship. In the end, your discernment will choose what is useful or applicable in the moment.

Focus on the principles within the tools and techniques.
Use and apply them *consistently,* not constantly.

Tools are used to support your attention and have that attention become integrated. Eventually this integration will serve as its own reminder or prompt from your inner sense in response to the outer situations. The external tools, thinking of rebalancing, looking at the photo of your favorite mountain, the lovely rock on your desk will pulsate as concrete reminders. But more deeply, by giving them focus and training your attention in certain directions, you are creating a deeper attitude of *attunement* that will serve as your own reminder without the actual sayings, symbols, etc.

Our client felt the allergy metaphor useful. He said, "I can see now that certainly the body has all of these natural functions when it encounters some undesired thing and it makes sense that the energetic system would have a similar type of reaction."

Consider that the body *is* going to make use of what it already knows. It may use the power of aggression and anger, for example, because it is trying to get rid of energy; to *push it away.* It makes sense to that aspect of the body/mind. What do little kids do when they are upset or frightened? Sometimes they cry and withdraw. Other times they get tough and push, saying, "Get away from me." The mind learns these aggression patterns and sees them as direct and useful responses. In addition, anger is sometimes a necessary and balanced point of movement. An angry outburst may be what is required to communicate and effect a useful and positive change.

> The continuing reminder is to keep your conceptual
> models broad and be willing to change them.

Can you look at aggression neutrally as a natural expression? If so, you then have an opening to finding *another* expression. Can you see depression as a message for rest and renewal, rather than a stab of fear that you are not coping well enough? Can you see over-responsiveness as a learned pattern and allow yourself inner permission to be less responsive to others in a balanced way? The intense receptivity of empath nature tends to amplify responses to that which is unconsciously and subconsciously sensed and felt. All the tools, techniques and principles are ways to expand your understanding of yourself; acknowledging and accepting your possibilities and limits as well. Recognizing a limit can be as useful as actualizing a dream. Allow yourself *all* the realms of being that come present in your life.

Although that which is unconscious can impact us negatively or impede our awareness, you can harness the power of the unconscious. In considering a conceptual base and applying focus and attention, you are consciously internalizing tools to serve you clearly, quickly and more automatically in the future. In this way, you are working in partnership with your unconscious aspect and through that partnership, you operate from a more integral perspective.

Choices, actions, and reactions are often the
outgrowth of unconscious empathic connection –
with yourself as well as others.
Use discernment and differentiation as an ally
to see, and therefore experience,
the world more clearly.

CHAPTER THREE

ON RELATING

The sense of being part of a collective
is a prominent awareness for empaths.
In this reality, the separate individual
is the dominant paradigm.
Finding the balance of these differing
perspectives is essential.

The energy of the empath is where communication and connection are most often one and the same. It is essentially energy of a *collective* nature, where being with each other is a natural extension of being with oneself. It is a collective nature where being with and communicating with each other is felt as a linking, merging and *knowing* of oneself and others. It is energy and connection experienced as a visceral, physical flow of exchange, not bound by conceptualization and language. The communication medium is energy itself, as in an extension of the self akin to an aura. Empaths extend, flow and connect with each other. In such connection, there is a gestalt – a *wholeness* of recognition, understanding and exchange. Empaths experience an ebb and flow of connection and communication.

While empaths can sense and tap into deep awareness of being part of a collective, the separate individual is the focal point of this reality. It is essential for empaths to balance these different and seemingly opposite perspectives. Ideas of connection and flow in a collective represent an extraordinary intimacy. There are few current cultural-social structures that support the kind of intimate communication exchanging *energy* would facilitate. Rather, communication is experienced as distant, using language, not a direct energy flow. Certain ranges of behavior are allowed to become more intimate, where simply "feeling" the other is expressed. This is evident in physical sexuality or the care and feeding of infants, but in general there is a limited range of energetic intimate connection. Such connections have layers upon layers of social and cultural limitations and taboos, all of which tend to inhibit, rather than foster direct exchange of energy as communication.

In many cultures it is still unusual to accept that one could sense or feel or understand that which has not been said, yet this is a typical empath experience. You "pick up" things. You hear undercurrents in language. You hear someone saying something to you and you get the sense of what is going on, of what is meant and felt. Often they may have been in touch with what you sense and recognize it once you've shared your sense. "Reading" someone's mind is felt as invasive and unacceptable, and to some, frightening or evil. Such a capacity certainly isn't seen as simply another way of hearing or sensing more than language, and yet this communication experience is typically a core element of the empath experience.

A continuing challenge for the empath is *balance*. One asks, "How do I balance? How do I work with this? How do I cope with my abilities to sense things when other people don't know they are communicating this way and disagree with me. How do I make sure that what I am picking up is in fact what is being said?" These very questions are the vital first step toward balance. They recognize that you must bring attention and discernment to your responses before taking action or settling on your interpretation.

A balancing factor is found in separating your sense of reception from the accuracy of your interpretation.

Empaths do receive, but that is no guarantee that in each instance you accurately or fully understand what you receive. When you allow receiving and interpretation to be considered separately, you will find more ease in being a receptive person. You will also be more able to not feel the need to attach to the accuracy of your interpretation or expand the importance of your sensing. Consider information received with discernment and be willing to let go of your first interpretation. Allowing separation of reception and interpretation often increases the flow of receptivity, as it is not burdened by the need to be correct. This kind of balance also supports others in being more comfortable supporting your receptivity. They will not feel encumbered by having to accept your interpretations of everything, perhaps laden with an attitudinal authority of "I sensed it, so it must be true."

Understanding your nature and seeing that it is different asks you to be conscious, responsible and accountable.

Empaths often hold the sense that "I am connected to and am rooted somewhere other than where I am now." Empaths often do not accurately translate this sense of otherness. You must also ask, "I feel this is the empath way, but does it work in my here and now? Do I need to modulate or modify it or look at it again?" By using this simple reference system of asking and inquiring, you can use language to build your personal history of reference and recognition. Questions create language bridges between your conscious awareness and your sensing awareness. When you ask, "This is what I innately want to do, is this the empath way and does it work here now?" you are connecting your conscious *discerning* awareness to your innate *sensing* awareness. One person distilled such questions into her personal catch-phrase, *"Empath way or Earth way?"*

Remember, empath awareness often needs to be transduced and translated. Again, one must always be responsible to the consideration that your interpretation of what you receive may not be wholly accurate or be appropriate to act upon. You may experience this need to question and doubt as frustrating, but it is essential. It is incumbent upon *you* to know how you operate and how your difference may affect other people. You may gather a cadre of like-minded people around you where you feel free-flowing and unfettered, but on the whole most of your interactions will be with people *not* like you. People will then say you are too sensitive, too emotional, too different, too, too, *too*; essentially declaring, "You are other than me. You are not like us." Such statements may be an accurate reflection of their feelings.   The fuller truth is that you are *exactly* as intense and emotional, as sensitive and receptive, as you need to be to express your empath nature. Although people may indeed feel you are operating at an intensity and velocity, a depth and density, that is hard for *them*, you must always hold to "Yes, I understand it is hard for you, but it's perfectly in accord for *me*."

In a workshop, a woman said, "My frustration comes from how I perceive people and it's too much sometimes and I feel I lose myself. My way of coping has been to distance myself from people and situations. Yet, a part of me says I can find a better way."   Sometimes distancing oneself *is* the most direct and effective thing to do. Recognizing, "I can't do this. I don't want to be here now. I not going to deal with this situation." can be the accurate choice. But as she says, need this be the only option? Setting boundaries is a valuable tool.   Empaths usually resist boundaries; linked to the sense that empath collectives are places of merged energies without boundary. Some empaths have shared images of realities where the collective is physically connected in a form similar to a sea anemone, with the individual fronds having a common root.

> It is your responsibility to yourself and others
> to learn, acknowledge and accept
> your own limits and boundaries.

When you find yourself using distance to balance, are you avoiding taking on the responsibility of setting limits and boundaries? Are you stepping back from fear of confrontation or conflict?   Ask such questions and recognize that your first response may not be the most effective response. "Ah, no boundaries is what I innately flow to do; but is it workable with this person?" Your own boundaries are essential in a reality where most others operate with boundaries. They will not easily recognize the ebb and flow of your energy and thus may be moved to take more from you, waiting for *you* to set the limit. Without limits, empaths quickly feel over-extended; as if all your energy flows out without return or exchange. Others may not be attuned to ebb and flow, to exchange and the movement of energy in the way you are. They will look to *you* for the clues of what is enough and what you require.

Often friends, family and co-workers simply do not understand what happens to you and wonder at your exhaustion. They will say to you, "Well, I didn't ask you to do that. Why didn't you just say you didn't want to? Why didn't you just say no?" They are correct in their defense since they sense your underlying assumption that they should have recognized your depletion. Their assumption is that you will declare your own limits as they do. The empath dilemma is that you don't easily say no because you are caught in the sense that you should respond to another's need or desire of your help and energy. You *know* that person needs you. You see, sense and feel it. You must learn that although you *can* see or *can* know, this does **not** mean it is your cosmic responsibility to *act* upon all that you know or give what you sense is needed. Such over-arching responsiveness is simply not possible or useful to everyone involved.

Ultimately, it is your responsibility to learn, acknowledge and accept your own limits and set boundaries. It is also essential that you let go of any empath *shame* about setting limits and saying no. People often carry a deep sense of shame that they can't extend their energy to everyone or be there whenever people need them. Empaths carry the innate feeling to respond, transmute, and change the energy and when they cannot, they feel they have failed, as if they are out of integrity.

To cope with empath shame, use the tool of reference.
Place feelings of failure and wrongness in a context.
Grow comfortable with what you can and cannot do.

Reference asks you to be willing to examine your feelings more neutrally, to place them in a context and then see what they may *refer* to. Place the situation in a context by recognizing, "I have a movement to do something that I really can't do here and now." Further referencing questions help you more accurately identify your feelings. "Am I compelled? Am I afraid? Am I moved to do what I have always done?" Finding as accurate an understanding as you can helps you disengage from your first reaction, which then gives you an opening to consider what else you may choose to do. Empath shame is exacerbated by being unwilling to accept your limits. You must grow comfortable in recognizing what you can and cannot do.

As you do so, you are also learning how to share yourself in ways that are useful and balanced. You can learn to say, "I'm really here for you. I've enjoyed talking with you, but you know, we've been on the phone for an hour and I really can't talk to you any further right now.

I've got to go." Such phrases serve as *language bridges*, where words hold to the *essence* of a situation, not necessarily the specifics. When you say, "I have to get off the phone now because I am really feeling a little tired," or "I need to get off the phone now because I've got to focus on something else," you are letting them know your limit in a clear statement. You are sharing your tiredness or other commitment, but are not making it specific to the person you are speaking with. By sharing the tenor of your core feelings in an open-ended way, other people can receive the message and allow themselves to shift in response. The openness of essence versus specific allows people to shift positions more easily and more neutrally. Ambiguous messages easily lead to misinterpretations and assumptions.

Language bridges serve as an archetype of your intent; phrases that reflect the essence of your thought.

Choose words and phrases that serve as a bridge to another person and truly share ideas and concepts. Language bridges hold the essence of a situation and serve as an archetype of one's intent. Words are selected with the intent to *allow* people to shift rather than demanding agreement. Using neutral language enhances the process. "I think you must do this action with me as I know it is correct," is a forceful statement of your opinion and your will. When you say, "It is important to me that we take this action, as after all I've learned, it seems the correct thing to do," you create a bridge to the other person. In sharing the feeling that the action is important to *you,* that you have learned about it and that it "seems" right, the other person may respond in kind. When you share that you have learned, it opens the way for them to ask what you learned; saying that the action "seems" right, also leaves the door open for their input.

Even if you are not open to changing the outcome, you can still use language bridges to communicate the essence of your intent. Thus, you can say, "This action seems essential and very important to me, so I am letting you know that this is what I am going to do." In this, the other person may see that although there is no option for them to prevent you from taking the action, they may resonate with the key words of "essential" and "very important" and accept your *feeling* about the action, even if begrudgingly.

The more you are willing to set the limits, the more easily you can *express* the limits to others. The more willing you are to express limits, the more you are able to hold them. People who are uncomfortable with setting their own limits are also unwilling to accept responsibility for them. Rather than stating clearly their limits, they often use degrees of anger to push another person away. They declare, "You've exhausted me. I've got to go now." By blaming the other, you are avoiding being responsible for yourself. You are placing responsibility on others to recognize your needs. While that may satisfy the part of yourself uncomfortable with setting boundaries, it also gives away your own power to direct your life.

> It is your responsibility to learn which
> tools and approaches work best for you.
> Within the acceptance of this responsibility is
> self-authority, empowerment and strength.

The task of the empath *is* to recognize the requirements of your reality, even when you feel them as limitations. What you can extend and give *energetically* is simply not the same as what can be done physically. When you allow yourself to say, "I'm sorry, I'm just weary," you are sharing clarity. Each time you do not honor the truth of your need, you will have to cope with it. Give yourself permission to say no. Take on the ability to respond to *yourself,* as in "I can't do that." Accept being the guardian of your own empathic nature.

Empaths over-extend because they relate by tuning in and merging energetically. What is forgotten is that empath energy can easily outrun your physical energy. The empath energy system is of a higher, deeper velocity and intensity. You must work *with* the physical and use your mind as the guardian to set up structures that support the physical. Structures and boundaries support you in expressing your empath nature in a comfortable and blossoming way.

As you have noticed, the "crash and burn" approach of coping with life can be exhausting. Simply retreating is not the answer either, because then you feel lonely and disconnected. Retreating can also invoke shame in feeling you are *unwilling* to extend your energy. What is required is your willingness to recognize when you are hitting your limit or the need to set a limit on extending your energy. Finding where to set boundaries is not difficult because people usually clearly recognize when they overdo and what those situations are. The challenge is giving yourself *permission* to set boundaries beforehand or recognize the need to set a limit in the moment, particularly when you are being asked to respond to someone else's need.

Another difficulty for empaths is the comparison between "this is how it is done and this is how I do it." As you become clearer about how *you* operate, you will find the language bridges that resonate with empath energy; choosing words that best describe your feelings. Thus, you can simply say, "I am feeling emotionally exhausted today, so I am not able to do what you've asked." The emotional clarity in this statement leaves no ambiguity that you are saying no. The person can hear the truth of your sense of yourself, which also keeps the energetic door closed to their challenging or renegotiating your response. This complements setting boundaries and creating external structures that support you.

> It is essential for you as an empath to be willing
> to release the outcome of what you sense.
> It is the right and responsibility of others to make
> their own discernment about what you might share.

When you say to a friend, "You know, I get a sense that you might want to think about this in a different way," they may not get the same sense at all and may even have a negative reaction. Don't immediately react to their response. Pause a moment and hold your own energy within yourself. When you feel you can *respond*, rather than react, you can share, "It works for me like this. Sometimes I just tune in and pick things up." In this way you are explaining your process, but not defending the information. As you hold your own energy and offer your willingness to share, you accept the responsibility of being clear about how and what you sense. By sharing your process but not expecting them to agree with your interpretation, you also open the door for them to discover how to tune into themselves in a similar way. Do not accept responsibility for the actions of others in response to what you share. As importantly, you must also be comfortable when others do *not* understand your process, do not agree with your perspective and are not interested in following your example or suggestions. Allow their own discernment of the information.

The goal is to become centered in yourself, so you are not defensive about what you sense and how it is received.

You are always sharing by example. Empaths have heightened receptive and responsive abilities, but most other people can touch into empathic *qualities* -- sensitivity, receptivity, linking within, connection and so on. Like a gifted musician with perfect pitch, you can share and teach others *about* music, even though they may not have the musician's great ability. As you come to understand the nature of yourself with a degree of otherness and embrace your difference, you can let go of wanting to be like those you are different from. Conversely, embracing the Other within allows you to be more accepting of those who are not like you. Acknowledging that you can feel a sense of "Us and Them" does not stratify or separate. Rather it says, "Ah yes, there is difference and by acknowledging that difference, you can allow connection *just as it is available.*" You can let go of comparison to how else we think others should be.

Balancing can feel like frustration. What *is* frustration? It is usually energy that wants to flow in one channel and finds that it cannot be expressed through that channel. Frustration is energy that seeks one path, a certain direction and finds it is blocked. At times it is accurate that the energy *cannot* flow in the direction you desire. Dance with empath energy, rather than coping with it. When you get to those frustration points, remember "This pathway seems blocked. Is there another option?" Allow another way to express the energy.

Being an empath brings intensity and vitality to your life, a heightened awareness very few of you would like to give up. What you want to give up is the *awkwardness* of your empath dance. The way to *allow* this awkwardness to shift and change is to hear the music and rhythm of your empath nature more clearly. Find ways for the beat of your culture and the rhythm of your nature to flow more easily together.

> Move toward an *integral* expression of your nature.
> Hold the idea of integral not as a static oneness,
> but as a dancing, moving flow.

Your dance sometimes feels as if it emerges from competing foundations of knowledge and awareness; your empath nature in uncomfortable juxtaposition with every day life. Is the dance classical ballet or hip hop? Instead, think of life's dance as *improvisation*. Listen and respond to the music of the moment. Tune into the idea that you are energy moving as both the particle and the wave. From this perspective, frustration can be seen simply as a *signal*; "Ah, I need to find another way. I need to change the beat and change my tune."

Empaths find it very difficult for issues between individuals or situations to stay unresolved.

A continuing dilemma for many empaths is the desire for *resolution*. In an empath culture nothing can stay unresolved or unaligned. Unresolved energy would vibrate within the Collective. The movement would be to take any dissonant vibration and let it *flow* until it was comprehended, understood and the energy came into alignment, which is resolution. Keep in mind that in an empath reality, energy is modified, transmuted and changed in a methodology not readily available to you. It is as if the vibrations themselves have rhythm, velocity and intensity. Many people picture empath reality as like everyday reality, but extremely psychic and sensitive. It is an *entirely* different modality of expression. Modulation and resolution would happen in a type of energetic physical exchange. At times you do experience resolutions through non-verbal means, such as meditation, movement like Yoga or Tai Chi and other practices.

On the whole, though, language is the primary mode of relating and communication. Collective energy is carried within the individual. Alignments and resolution are reached through language and concepts, such as "let's work it out." Empath culture reaches resolution through energetic movement that leads to a gestalt of knowingness. You may see reflections of this perspective in how you relate to others, but it can *only* be a reflection. Keeping this difference in mind supports staying free of the comparison of otherwhere and the present.

The innate empath sense is that
all challenges have solution.
All conflicts have resolution.

This sounds like a wonderful goal and approach. But the ideal that all challenges have solution and all conflicts have resolution is not innate to the nature of this reality. Sometimes the real goal of resolution and solution is finding a way for the energy to be expressed. Paradoxically, this may occur without *direct* resolution or solution of the *direct* situation with the person or the environment. The pull for resolution makes it extremely frustrating when you come upon a situation you *cannot* impact or resolve. You feel the limitation where your energy cannot be expressed. Empaths forget to question if resolution is essential or possible. They often tend to focus on the block itself. Remember, many others *can* flourish with unresolved situations. Finally, there are many situations that are not yours *to* resolve. You are not given the tools, the position, the opportunity or the right to bring resolution.

When you come to those situations when a person doesn't want to talk to you, doesn't want to talk about what happened and work it out or when it's a situation that is not left to you to resolve -- remember that the movement toward resolution and solution is *yours* and not necessarily theirs. If you continue to return to the same passageway with the same approach – "we must resolve this" – remember the blockage is what *you* are feeling.

Understanding how empath precepts influence you
gives you more tools to see yourself in a fuller context.

Integrating empath precepts allows discernment of the moment to become clear. In resolution, it is helpful to understand that a part of you wants everything resolved because without resolution, you feel isolated and disconnected from the collective you strongly sense. At times it is most helpful to put aside the situation and your desire for resolution. You can make a gesture *towards* resolution at a distance. by sending a card or email. If that gesture still brings no response, accept it. Dance with the energy and situation as it is. Discover the strength that comes from tolerating your unease and discomfort with situations you are not given to effect. Your impetus to resolve and solve, may seem like a wholly positive force, but resolution is not always available as an action and more so, is not always the *aligned* option. Some people and situations learn through the disruption that can only emerge when things are *not* solved or resolved. Clarity and growth come through many paths.

In some unresolved situations, friends may advise you to just get angry or respond in kind. Empaths often cannot follow that approach. Their energy does not easily align to holding emotional locked doors. The possibility of connection and reconnection and the permeability of relating feel more present. Yet, there are times when it is essential to *close* the door and *not* move toward a person or situation. You can allow your willingness to open the door at another time, but the true alignment of a situation can also be *accepting* a boundary or limit and an unresolved connection.

Empaths hold deeply the possibility of transformation.

A client shared her conflict with a challenging friendship that ended with much difficulty. "But I can't just cut her out of my life!," she cried. She could not make that choice, but she could put the relationship aside, "up on the shelf". Empaths strongly hold a deep sense of shifts and change and transformation. If in the future, the once-friend had a car accident and called to say, "I had a near death experience and you are the only person who would understand" – no matter what had happened earlier, she and most empaths would say, "All right, tell me about it."

What empaths experience as a compelling capacity to reconnect and respond does not drive other people in the same way. Another person might say, "Forget it. Go find somebody else," and hang up the phone. Other people can close chapters of their lives and not hold any connections from that past. Allow yourself to clearly see all the variations in relating. Recognize your own capacities, with their strengths and weaknesses, and do not judge or misread others actions. It is essential that you *recognize* that their choices may not mean the same thing or have the same emotional impact on them as it would to you. You truly may *not* understand how they make their choices.

You may not want to slam the emotional door and lock it, but leaving the door ever open is not always useful. This choice leaves you holding all the energy, flowing outward with no return; there is no ebb in the flow. Instead, acknowledge the truth of the situation to yourself.

"This is very frustrating for me. I hate these situations, but they do come up. Here are my feelings about what has happened. It hurts me and I'm sad, frustrated and I don't know what to do." Put *all* your feelings out on the table. Don't try to talk yourself out of your feelings. Don't try to match a comparison to some ideal of how a person *should* handle the feelings. Just stay with what the feelings are and then take those cards, if you will, tie them in a little ribbon and put them on the shelf. You know they are there. If you look at them again, it might still hurt. You might not reach resolution as you desire, but by acknowledging your true feelings and setting further *action* about them aside, you are not denying your feelings to reach a false completion. You are leaving the door unlocked, but not open. If that person calls again, you may talk to them. You probably will.

With this approach, even when an unresolved situation still hurts, energy will flow around it and keep moving. Many empaths often do not let go and find that hurt feelings are still intense years after the actual event; as if they have frozen and encapsulated their feelings. Energy does not stay the same and you will never return to those frozen moments exactly as they were. If the situation is revisited, it will be in the present moment and will include all that occurred to you and the other since your last meeting. Grow comfortable with the fact that life will move, shift and change as it will. In the end, you will always have the option to reconsider and respond anew.

It is essential for empaths to allow themselves to be
clear about their own feelings without judgment.

Empaths tend to "handle" their feelings and use many ways to do so,
such as denial, repression, rationalization, looking to the future or
greater good, and telling themselves all will be well no matter what.
Typically, they have done so from a very young age. Sometimes this
was a protection formed in a difficult childhood. At other times, it is a
version of the empath way of understanding. As an example, an
empath child has something happen to them. It hurts and saddens
them, but because they can so easily perceive and understand the *other*
person's feelings and the whole of the situation, the child quickly
moves towards resolving and solving. When the child feels the flow
of helping and solving energy, he feels competent and safer in a
difficult situation.

When an empath is trying to make resolution and people do not
respond or understand what one is striving toward and events are not
resolved, the empath feels compromised and afraid. You may feel,
"Oh, I'm the one who always has to be understanding because I see
more of the picture than the other person." The other person might
actually expect that from you because they have accepted the role you
often present, as the one who gives, compromises and finds the win-
win situation.

*Responsibility means respond-ability - the ability to respond.
It does not mean there is a cosmic mandate upon you
to respond to each and every situation.*

There is another kind of boundary you need to explore and allow. This boundary is anchored in what many empaths experience as a deep capacity to perceive and understand the motivations, needs, choices and actions of others. The sense of this capacity is typically accompanied by a feeling that is your *responsibility* to respond to others as needed. Such a capacity does *not* mean you *have* to cope with or give others what they need or want. Recognizing that you are not *compelled* to respond is a consistent challenge for empaths, as it pushes against your innate willingness to respond. The key-word to focus on is *willingness*. Willingness is what you can *choose* to offer, not what you are compelled to do. Further, you can see responsibility as respond-ability, an *ability* to respond. Like willingness, an ability is something you can choose to offer. Allow yourself to develop a comfort level of understanding a situation without taking action. Consider that the true balance and harmony of the situation may involve holding others accountable for their own actions. Consider that the truer responsibility might be to yourself in learning to *not* respond if it is costly and out of balance for you to do so.

*Unexpressed and unexamined emotions become encapsulated
and wrapped in the unfulfilled energy of resolution and solution.
These feelings become literal cocoons, holding feelings inside.*

Empaths experience many situations throughout their lives where they leap to understanding and resolution. There is an element of *denial* in such leaps. Empaths are moved by their impetus to resolve and overlook any conflicting or paradoxical elements in their choice of action. The movement to help is satisfying and pleasurable and often empaths do not want to deny that satisfaction by questioning the moment. The situation is further compounded by the tendency to deny and talk themselves out of their feelings. This results in layers of unexpressed and unacknowledged emotions.

Young empath children are very in touch with their ability to understand and are cognizant on many levels of the interplay of emotions in a family. These children extend and give energy to the family, moving toward understanding and resolution. The empath child offers energy to be used in change and transmutation. In the course of this, the child may have feelings of their own – fears and hurts or concerns and confusions – that get encapsulated in energy and cocooned. These feelings have not been transmuted, expressed and released. Instead they are nestled within the psyche as unexpressed, repressed and unconscious or subconscious patterns. These energy patterns are part of what is engaged when you refer to having your "buttons pushed." Situations where you are oversensitive or find challenging are another echo of the cocoons. Sometimes you can recognize the connection from a current reaction to a past event; at other times such awareness is not available to you. Early cocoons are created from a child's experience of the world, left to them to understand and manage.

Life is a series of transcending events, forming hierarchal layers of identities. As one grows, you move on to another layer of identity, always *including* where you have already been in life and your earlier identities.   Unrecognized, challenging and painful events that are pushed aside and cocooned, do not become integrated with the evolving whole. Cocoons continue to be created each time you are unwilling to examine your choices, leap over your confusions or hide from your true feelings.

> The unexpressed sits within us waiting to be acknowledged;
> hiding, reacting and motivating us in many ways.

A useful process for most people, but especially for empaths, is a time of review, putting the "cards on the table." You can do this generally or specifically.   When something occurs that really pushes your buttons, sit down with a paper and pencil and ask, "What is this connected to? What is going on? What unexpressed feelings am I holding? What *cocooned* feelings are here?" and see what arises. In this process you are trying to just discover and allow the feelings to be expressed to yourself. You are *not* trying to understand them, resolve them or make a solution.

Sometimes cocoons are very old, linked to times when you made strategies and solutions, but did not allow yourself to recognize and feel your pain. What you did not do was cry or be angry or feel afraid. When you talk about the situation now, you say, "My mother abused me, but she was such an abused person herself, I just feel compassion for her." And you really do feel that and it is part of the whole truth, yet also present is that little boy or girl who "understood" everything away. You are still the child who did not express all your feelings and now does not let the adult-self feel the depth of those same feelings. In your willingness to ask and inquire, you can access the truth held within the cocoons and free the flow of emotion.

Since many cocoons are formed in the earliest years, the energy is often held as pre-verbal emotion.

A tool to access these feelings is what we call the Heart Bear. Children are attracted to stuffed animals because they connect to the iconic and archetypical energy held in the idealizations of animals. Thus lions are courageous, monkeys are clever, and bears are protectors and great mothers. These qualities are evident in animal myths and tales around the world and in ancient times. The children also find comfort in the idea that the animal is different than a person, separate from the actual people in their lives and representing a connection to other worlds and other realms.

Find a soft and cuddly stuffed animal you are attracted to that will serve as your symbolic Heart Bear. Lie down in a comfortable place and hold the bear to your chest. Holding the intent that you are going to allow a release of emotion, visualize that the bear is caring and comforting and able to absorb and transmute any and all emotion. Let yourself drift with this feeling and allow whatever response may arise. This approach sometimes takes a bit of time. Be giving and gentle with yourself. Many people report strong releases of energy, including crying, deep sobs and sadness. The Heart Bear unconditionally accepts the energy and offers comfort in return. You may also find that the Heart Bear can continue to serve this purpose, just as it may have done when you were a child. Find a special place for your Heart Bear to be present in your space.

Let the situations of your life lead your inner discovery.
Follow the inquiry when the moment arises.

When confusion or pain and fear arise, let yourself sit and bring your attention to what is present. See what you can reveal to yourself. Allow the feelings to come up and out. You can draw them with colors. You can talk them out. You can cry them out or you might just sit numbly with them. There are so many ways to let emotions be expressed, to find another path for the frustrated, stopped energy. The unseen and unfelt has impact and influence. In the cocooned feelings and blockages, you are being impacted by unrecognized pressures.

Empaths require their energy to flow and move; it is their emotional breathing This is a bit like sharks who must swim constantly to breathe; the motion of swimming creates a water flow through the gills that facilitates oxygenation. Cocooned energy builds up and sits like heavy, sodden weights; limiting your emotional breath. This emotional weight drains the physical body, like having an undercurrent fever impacting your emotional immune system with a cumulative effect. The unseen and unrecognized cocoons need to be discovered and acknowledged. When you bring your acknowledgment and attention to these stored hurts, you create a fresh energy flow, that will lighten the heavy feelings and begin a movement toward release on its own. You do *not* need to consciously resolve or fulfill every wound or issue. At times your only option will be to simply acknowledge the feelings and set action about them aside. "I feel this way about this situation and there is nothing I can do about it. So I am going to put it aside."

> Do not judge yourself for what you
> have not seen or understood.
> Allow yourself to proceed from, "I see this *now*."

To further understand what may surround emotional and physical problems, begin a review, creating an inventory from a flow of free-associative questions. Ask, "What do I not know about? What do I not see?" Inquiry and acknowledgement often initiate shifts and changes in the body. You might lose weight, headaches may lift, digestion may improve and so on. Be clear to not judge yourself with "I should have seen that. I should have known. How could have I missed that?" This is another expression of empath shame. Having empath nature does not mean all energy is visible and clearly understood. A great percentage of life is asking you to focus out *there,* not within. And a great percentage of the culture says, "Handle this. Deal with this. Get rid of that." Don't attach to what was not seen or understood. Bring it to your attention, look at it and address it now.

You can do inquiry processes on your own or with a friend. Set them in motion by saying, "I want to know what things are going on with me. I am willing to see what comes up." You have asked the question, now *allow* the response. Responses may not come in the moment of asking the question. Perhaps they will arise when you are driving along or doing the dishes. Allow these things to "pop up" in their own time and place. You will soon discover your own patterns of question and response. You can then let the feelings be seen and then allow yourself to experience and *feel* the feelings. They may lighten or change and transmute. If not, you can acknowledge them and place them on the shelf. In any event, through inquiry, energy is no longer hidden, unexpressed and cocooned.

> Inquiry takes many forms, including,
> "I sense something is going on,
> but right now I cannot be present with it."

In a workshop, a woman wonders about exploring these cocoons. "You know I've been dealing with my illness and I feel all these emotions coming up. I don't feel I can address them now, but think I should try to."

The principle of inquiry can be pursued while honoring that you are stressed by your current situation. An open-ended line of inquiry could go like this, "And when it is a good time, I'd like to know what this was connected to." It may be that the literal information is not the point. Since your body is actually eliminating waste from your treatments, you may simply and literally be detoxing. You can ask, "Is there anything else to be learned here? I'd like to know what this is related to." If you are really comfortable, you could just say, "Just transmute and let it go. And maybe I'll know about it later."

Frame your inquiry from the truth of where you are in the moment. When you are aware an issue is present, but don't feel able to examine it, you are still *acknowledging* that which is unexpressed and held within the cocoons. You may want to know what the feelings are connected with. At times specific knowledge is not available or events are not directly related to the feeling. Energy can become captured with unexpressed feelings. The emotions are no longer linked to one thing, which leaves no clear or direct association.

The woman who was ill and detoxing had a non-specific association to her sense that "something was going on." In this case, nothing came up in *language* because she was holding unexpressed energy *per se*, not what the emotions were rooted in. A direct association or link was not available. It is as if it were stored on her inner hard drive, but the directory isn't linked with the data anymore. If one can acknowledge this may be so, one can allow feelings to just be felt and heard and perhaps released. Referencing to time and place and specific events is not essential to uncovering the feeling. Self-inquiry may also lead to a deeper process where you may seek a counselor for ongoing inquiry with a neutral observer who can offer insight and support.

On boundaries and connection, another woman associated to her work as a massage therapist. "I expand myself out and with so many different clients; they take me to a dimension I haven't even considered before. I find myself staying linked with my clients after the sessions. I'm comfortable with that because I feel with my being an empath we will always be linked energetically. They come back for a session and say I was with them in their meditation. I believe them, but I'm not doing that consciously. This feels okay, but a part of me wonders if it is always okay; should I set some boundaries on this?"

Remember, empath reality is primarily *energetic* reality. When you feel connected to empath reality, you are linking to the *energy* of another place. This reality, *your* reality, is solid and physical. If you want to place a boundary to create balance, remember to link it to the physical. Set limits on how you receive energy. Use an object as a physical symbol of this limit. When you are not willing to set boundaries, eventually the physical energy is not going to match the empath vibration and situations arise where the physical will require your attention. Perhaps you will become drained or irritable as your clients intermingle with your energy. Energetic and emotional connections are actual links from which you can experience a direct physical effect. Empath energy is of a different velocity than the physical. The physical world needs to be accommodated by empath energy with modulation and limits.

Our massage therapist is talking about allowing certain energetic links with her clients to stay in place. She has trusted that her empath nature knows how to operate and is comfortable with her choice, since she sees these connections as in an energetic realm. In her question, she is also considering, "Can I fully set this in motion without thinking about it or connecting it with this physical reality?" It is essential to be consciously aware of the connections you invite and allow and it would be balancing to add an energetic boundary. "I honor the connection. I allow this connection in my work as long as it is harmonious and in balance for both my empath and physical nature." Keeping yourself all-open can literally drain the physical body. You find days you don't feel refreshed from sleeping or nights filled with unremembered dreams. These may not be your *own* experience. Even when you feel very connected to the collectives of other people or otherwheres, those collectives are not operating at the same wavelength as the physical self. These are energetic connections that are understood only to a degree. Be conscious of your choices and act as the guardian of your physical self and of the requirements of the body's energy system.

Although your empath nature *can* reach out and extend, the body operates within physical law. The body needs REM sleep, time for processing food and cellular changes and growth; time for renewal. You can interfere with these vital processes by overextending your energy. Tiredness, irritability, increased emotional sensitivity are signs that you are out of balance energetically. When another's need becomes so strong it impacts your physical being, set a boundary. Include boundaries within your intent by saying, "I am open to this connection, but if it becomes draining or unbalancing, this link will close." You are establishing an energetic fail-safe or a circuit-breaker. The healer's first responsibility, *everyone's* first responsibility is the Guardianship of the Self, because when you are depleted you have nothing to extend to another and nothing left to support yourself.

> See limit-setting as a supportive structure,
> rather than as creating confining boundaries.

It is very seductive to extend energy and it makes the empath feel particularly alive. You feel the vitality of the expression of yourself, but you have to remember that your *energetic* capacity can far outreach the capacity of the physical. Energetic boundaries can serve as essential equipment and useful protection. They are a breathing apparatus for diving. They are your sunscreen. They are your arctic parka. Such limits and structures are you recognizing, "This is my physical reality and I must care for myself in it."

> Empath energy is not your primary or ascendant energy.
> Your physical and energetic systems are equal partners,
> working together with varying paces and timing.

Empath energy moves at a faster velocity than the body. It's as if you are a fast walker and your friend says "You're walking too fast for me." Thoughtfully, you slow down and match the pace of your friend. Once you get into the flow of walking, you unconsciously return to your *natural* pace. Your friend says, "You're getting ahead of me again," and you'll say, "Oh, I'm sorry" and try to match them once again. In just this way, your natural pace as an empath is faster than the pace of the body. When you unconsciously operate from empath energy you can easily not recognize when you are overextending the body. These different velocities of empath and physical energy will never *merge,* but dance in an interconnected partnership.

It is easy for empaths to be captured by the idealization that they are the only one who can help another. Everyone is part of the grand interconnection and support that is available in myriad ways through that interconnection. At times, you may be asked to be the one to step forward to another. At other times, they will find someone else, strength within or support from the All.

Balance living with empath energy and add to your well-being by:

- Setting in place structures of support.

- Allowing and setting boundaries.

- Leaving time for renewal.

- Balancing your desire for resolution.

- Exploring questions and inquiry.

- Bringing conscious attention to unexpressed energy.

- Finding balance between empath and physical energy.

- Remembering limits and boundaries as structures of support.

- Remembering you are but one source of support for others.

Empaths often feel their life should be 'holistic',
as in a single way or flow of being.
They struggle see what are they doing or not doing to
prevent experiencing this oneness in each situation.

Can you consider it may not be your own lack
that causes a situation, but a reflection
of the complexities of connection?

The words used to recognize the
underlying unity of existence ---
connected, aligned, resonating
do not mean Unity will manifest in an
unchanging singular flow of being.

CHAPTER FOUR

IN RELATIONSHIP

As you more fully recognize your empath nature,
you can allow yourself to relax into
relationships as they truly are.

Empaths often experience deep connection with others in a very short time. There is a strong sense of recognition and truly knowing someone. A paradox arises because at times this knowing soon feels complete, as if there is nothing left to explore, and you find yourself disconnecting from the relationship. Disconnection occurs when you are unconsciously operating from an empathic "merge" state. Merging can be seen in images of two people having their energy blend together; in images of minds linking and shared auras; in images of telepathy and shared dream experiences. Another image is of beings with an ability to become less solid and fluid; physically mingling and experiencing a gestalt of understanding and recognition of each other. They then separate and re-solidify, retaining the awareness they shared. You can see this imagery echoed in mystical fantasy and science fiction. These are all reflections of the idea of an empath reality with its capacity for complete energetic merging.

Considering the attraction of merging is useful in keeping your expectations and ideals grounded in what is available and possible. You may find you disconnect from others at inappropriate times and places as you unconsciously recognize the limits of merging; simply jumping out of relationship. As you more fully recognize your empath nature, you can allow yourself to relax into relating and relationships as they truly are and can be -- letting go of comparing them to unconscious and unattainable ideals.

Empaths tend to carry unexamined mental
ideals about partners and relationship.
Allow your ideas of relationship to evolve and mature
based on what is actually present in your life.

Empaths are rarely in relationship with someone matching their exact empathic nature. You might have friends who are empaths or have empath qualities, but they don't carry your same flow of energy. Sometimes empaths recognize each other and feel a sizzle of romantic connection. After a time the sizzle diminishes and friendship continues. Deep friendships and long lasting affinities are common between empaths. Empaths usually recognize and acknowledge each other when they first meet. In a romantic partnership, you may find yourself more attracted to energy that is different than your own, less familiar and new. Empaths carry an imperative to share their type of energy and are drawn to explore and connect with energy other than the familiar empath resonance.

You may carry a strong idealistic sense of what your future partner, that special person out there, will be like or what qualities they'll have. Often that ideal someone is an empath like yourself, but you find intimacy doesn't grow from the intense empath connection. Recognizing empath nature at play allows you to see these strong connections as a powerful link to another, but not the foundation for an enduring day-to-day relationship. Seeing this, you can discover arenas of relating that may not fit your subconscious model of relationship. Allow ideas of relationship to evolve more consciously from present times, rather than being rooted in echoes of otherwheres and otherwhens.

Empaths often are simply not aware that they experience or relate to others differently. To recognize these differences, it may be useful to think of yourself as choosing to live in another country and culture. You would consciously consider the culture you were in and act accordingly. You would choose your actions based on consideration of that culture. When you chose to go against the cultural norms, you would be aware that you might have to explain yourself or cope with negative responses. That is exactly what you have to do as empaths in general and especially in relationship.

Empaths often lament about relationship in this way, "I'd like to be in a relationship, but it doesn't seem to often work out with the people I am attracted to. I don't know what my relationships should be like or who to be with." When you share this with friends, they often respond with, "You're too intense, too sensitive, and too emotional. You either want to be too close or want too much space or both! You want too much, you give too much. You make people feel uncomfortable because you know what they're thinking." Following your empath impulses *unconsciously* can create a frustrating path.

There is a simple way to redirect your energy. Consider that you may *not* know just who or what you need in relationship. Question your empath impetus as the only way to respond. Be willing to say, "If what I am innately drawn to doesn't seem to work in my life, then let me meet someone who complements me in a way I don't anticipate and haven't figured out." More challenging, let this open, non-specific energy lead the way to relationship.

Embrace the principle of willingness. "I am willing to be receptive. I am willing to have connection. I am willing to have communication and we'll see where it goes." Let direct experience lead you, instead of ideas and ideals. Let the situation be led by how you actually relate to someone and more so, how others relate to *you*. All too often people move towards relationship as a task, an important and heavy goal that must be attained. Instead, engage with the attitude of play and let that lighter energy lead you. Let life as it comes lead the way. Be willing to relate to someone open-ended, without a goal. Let yourself explore connections and friendship comfortably, without worrying where the relationship is going or what it may evolve into.

Empaths often find relationships can be elusive.
Emotion and passion feel like an unfamiliar language.

Take the time to discover your own definitions of passion and emotion. Empaths may never feel totally merged in the customary ideas of human experience, thus the need to allow your own definitions of life. Discover the meaning of relating and connection based on your own experiences, as comparisons to the customary often do not reflect or support you.

Empaths must "come out" to themselves; acknowledging "There is always a part of me that feels connected to somewhere else. This feeling leaves me feeling slightly, sometimes *intensely,* disconnected from here." With such understanding, you can then begin inquiry into "How can *I* come to passion? How do *I* come to joy? How can I embrace relationship?" You can observe how it seems to be for others, but you must ask how is it for yourself. Reframing the question leads to reframing your understanding.

The unconscious expectation of and desire for merging pulls the empath. The desire to be merged does not seem like fantasy or fiction, but feels available and possible. No matter how true it may feel, one *cannot* have this exact experience. Merging in everyday life is couched in emotional tones and most often expressed in physical sexuality. In addition, while an empath may be drawn to merging, a fear often arises of being captured by it; of being literally trapped in the body of another. This is a defense that arises from unconscious experiences of this solid reality as different than an energy reality. In the present, emotion, spirit, and physicality are *interactive* as opposed to your sense of the innate merged integration of an empath realm. In many individuals the fear of merging has deepened into a powerful defense against emotional and physical connection. The very image of being trapped in form is a staple in science fiction and horror stories as well as in old myths and tales. These stories can be seen as a reflection of the possibility of such kinds of merging and co-mingling.

Understanding the push-pull of merging can free you to find comfort with the boundaries of this reality and also open you to the beautiful flow of intensity this capacity offers. When you are not clouded by longings for more or fettered by fears of entrapment, you can extend your energy and dance with all the merging that is available. Balanced empaths often experience a freedom of sexual expression, filled with intensity of connection and delight of experience. The merging capacity extends to all arenas of relating: connecting with infants and young children, linking to plants and animals, merging with nature in all its elements, communicating deeply with people who don't speak your language and more. Many empaths are travelers who are able to go into diverse cultures, using their empathic connection as communication.

**Many empaths develop the energy of the solitary traveler.
Empaths often have relationships that are atypical.**

Empaths often choose being solitary as protection against becoming emotionally depleted. Empaths seek a certain intensity of energetic exchange in their connections. When they feel the energy they receive does not match what they extend, they can feel depleted. Recognizing that this subconscious defense may be operating can make alignments feel more comfortable. Ask, "Am I really depleted or is this an internal fear? Can I find another way to be comfortable with others besides being alone?" As you consider how empath energy may influence you in what you are drawn to, in choosing and experiencing relationship, you can then wonder, "How can I be here in this body and experience connection and passion in the most wonderful balanced way I can?" Be willing to discover your own path. The capacity for awareness is always present. There are times one may not be sure how certain incidents are connected, but one registers them, notices their sequence and thinks about them. Conscious awareness of patterns can allow another perspective to present itself and take shape.

In relationship, empaths seek a
connection that adds to and takes them
further than their own energy.
This is passion.

Passion can take you beyond your own energy. It can move you beyond your own inhibitions, ideals and what you think about life. Passion is a coming together that creates still *another* energy. One wants to grow though connection and this is what draws you to relationship. Paradoxically, empaths are often concerned that the other will connect too much and want too much. They are often afraid the relationship will feel too settled and confining. Empaths experience themselves as more energetic than physical, and relationship highlights their ongoing paradox of not feeling the integration of the physical and energetic selves. This sense of being unconnected or disconnected can be projected onto the relationship.

The customary is often an imperfect model for the empath. Widen your concepts of how you can relate.

The customary may not serve as a complete model, but it is most useful to explore the *qualities* of the norm. "I want partnership. I want the transporting quality of a partnership. I want the energy that comes from a merged connection. I need separation. I have a fear of being captured in merged energy." Identify your assumptions in such statements and write them down. This is another inventory to help open cocooned fears and uncover hidden expectations and concerns. Be willing to not know and not yet have the answers. Initiate a process of *allowing* new awareness about relationship to come to you.

Some empaths are drawn to getting relationships settled. Unlike those who keep distance, they want to say, "Let me be with this person, so I can get a relationship anchored and I don't have to pay attention to searching any longer." They are waiting for the perfect person and the just right situation which is rarely met. Rather than wanting the ideal relationship, open to the idea that you are looking for energy and that it is found in other formats than a typical relationship. Consider the energy of connection as *encounters*. This might be a friendship with or without sexuality; a committed relationship – living together or separately, or a completely other frame of connection may develop in ways you have never considered. Open up and widen all your concepts of how one can relate.

Empaths typically see themselves as doing something
wrong in relationship, rather than questioning their
assumptions about the models they are operating from.

Empaths usually don't say, "It is very hard for me to find a life-long partner." Instead, they say, "I'm doing something *wrong* and when I get it straightened out, I am going to find the perfect partner." In addition, people rarely question the image of a life-long partner or wonder if it is the best situation for them. Empaths often experience an energetic completeness with their partner and at times, the constancy of day-to-day relationship begins to feel confining. Rather than leave the relationship, question its form and structure. Ask, "How can we be together comfortably?" Let yourselves evolve a structure of relating based on the truth and that really suits your needs, even though it may not echo the customary or your own ideal.

Where some empaths are seen as too emotional, others feel distance from others; seeming less connected and less emotional. This amplifies their desire for relationship and connection. This apparent distance and separateness can be a true characteristic or an adaptation to their heightened receptivity and the ability to know and merge. Again, begin with more clearly seeing what motivates and drives you and begin allowing new definitions. "I can allow how *I* am passionate to become clear to me." Ironically, many empaths consider their own intensity as *less* than the passion of others. Here is where unexamined inner definitions can become *limitations*. You can negate your own actual experience by saying, "No, that's not true passion; that's just intensity."

A limiting belief for many empaths is,
"I am more energetic than physical.
I am not a fully integrated person
like most people that I know."

Concepts can become poisonous limiting beliefs. Acknowledge your feelings and expand your ideas. Open your receptivity to the *qualities* of relationship -- connection and collaboration, giving and receiving, exchange and sharing. Allow yourself to discover and experience some of the myriad degrees and aspects of passion in life itself. Empaths can do well exploring a bit of energetic dating, rather than looking for that perfect partner. This dating is not the same as a partner or someone you live with, but it can be a connection where elements of intimacy and depth can grow. If the other person wants a deeper form like moving in together or marriage, before you do, acknowledge and accept the difference. Accommodating and giving what you truly cannot will only give you some time together, not a lasting relationship. On the other hand, acknowledging the differences can open up a compromise structure that supports both of you. Let yourself appreciate the relationship just as it is, "We are having this engaging relationship and although it might not go where other relationships go, it's all right just as it is."

Empaths often get into a cycle of approach and avoidance.
Feeling hurt is not something to avoid at all costs.

Empaths approach relationship with the fear of comparison and conflict. They are often sure that the other person will feel differently from them or want other things. They move into avoidance by thinking, "I shouldn't get into this relationship because the other person is going to be hurt by our differences," and they don't enter the relationship. This is a reflection of the self-idealized empath believing they are the one who understands and feels the situation. Let the other person be responsible for their *own* feelings. They're in it *with* you; they're attracted to it and you. They have the right to make their own choices and ride the currents of their life.

Another empath misconception is that feeling hurt is to be avoided at all costs. "Hurt" only means you have to cope with something. Taking the risk to be with people is worth opening to possible hurt. It is worth some hurt for you; it is worth some hurt for them. Hurt is another kind of energy. Hurt is also intensity and passion. To avoid hurt and therefore, to avoid all connection, is a waste.

> Do not abandon true experience waiting
> for idealized concepts to actualize.
> Be willing to live your life with passion and risk.

Empaths often choose to remain closed to others; all the while feeling, "Why am I alone?" They misguidedly take on what they perceive as the responsibility of a possible relationship. They say, "I can't get involved with this person because I am going to disconnect." Take the risk of being in a relationship as it is. Be willing to face shifts and changes when they actually arise. In that very moment, you will be able to see whatever action needs to occur. Do not hide from actual connection for fear of future loss and disconnection. Do not abandon true experience to wait for idealized concepts to actualize. Be willing to live your life with passion and risk. See risk as its own passion.

> It is essential to learn to discover and set
> caring, thoughtful parameters in relationship.

This refers to all relationships – intimate, professional, friends and family. Empaths often need support to find ease with setting the limits and boundaries. They need to learn to say yes and no, to discover their own clarity and to speak from it to explain and own their perspective. Empaths cope with their own pull to be all-available. Your capacity to give is easily recognized and naturally people want to receive what is being offered. It is your responsibility to set the parameters on your willingness to respond. You may struggle with the ease with which you can accommodate, especially in an ongoing relationship. Relationship is based on caring about and considering your partner's wants and needs, but to do so wholly you must be clear about your own. Be responsible for knowing and stating your needs. Learn to create useful, working boundaries.

Give yourself permission to hold structures of relationship that support you. These are not arbitrary, false structures, but those that evolve from listening to yourself and recognizing what you require. Also learn to see what moves you to override and abandon those very requirements. Create parameters based in as much clarity and awareness as you can summon. Ask your partner to explore these same considerations and together see what evolves as the workable, meaningful structure of your relationship.

In relationship, empaths often find they are
out-of-balance with their own needs
versus the needs of their partners and families.

Responding to and finding balance in relationship is a necessary quality, but empaths find the pull to respond to others overwhelmingly strong. The unconscious attunement to collective energy, the feeling of their expansive capacity to move energy and the feeling that they have time and availability for all possibilities contribute strongly to what can become a grandiose estimation of their capacity. By understanding that there *is* such a drive, you can remember to recognize when it is operating and take the moment to come present and question your inner-fueled *assumptions* of what is required. Reactions to unconscious patterns need to be addressed by everyone, but the situation is exacerbated for an empath.

When you really feel compelled or conflicted about
your response, this is a clue to pay attention.

Actions that are in alignment flow, even when there is compromise or letting go of your own intention. In the flow, it is clear to you on an inner and outer level, that you are *choosing* your action for the Whole. When you are left feeling contracted or conflicted, you have been given a useful clue that it is time to pause and be willing to examine your assumptions of what is truly the aligned action. It may be totally appropriate to say, "Not now. Can we do that later?" Empaths do not need to always adjust and accommodate, but so often *believe* this is required of them. Empaths leap to alleviate difficulty for others, often abandoning their own growth to do so.

*When your inner changes are challenging a relationship,
consider that things are different, not wrong.*

As you grow and change, many familiar and subconscious patterns end
up feeling awkward or problematic. When this feeling arises, rather
than worrying, ask, "Is this a problem or am I just doing it differently
now?" Give yourself a supportive context to consider what is going
on. "Is this a problem that needs to be examined or am I not yet
familiar with how I am doing this?" This allows you to walk with
awareness about your own shifts and changes. It is easier when you
embrace the concept that you are changing; that you are *within* change.
You can then begin to understand further *how* you are changing. As
with hurt and pain, stress and discomfort are not energies to be
avoided at all costs, for yourself or others. Rather, they are valid
energies of growth and movement. Empaths often are uncomfortable
in allowing others to accommodate them or asking them to do so.
When you are in a change-mode, other people recognize something
different is occurring and are usually quite willing to support you.

In a personal session, a woman shared that her adult stepson from a
former marriage sends her angry letters whenever she says no to
something he wants. She acknowledges that she has changed and is no
longer as responsive and accommodating to him as in the past. "I
usually wait before I respond to his letters and try to write while
feeling a connection to him, rather than reacting in anger. I would like
to just prevent the situation from happening. I feel I cannot just lash
out, but I get overwhelmed by his anger with me." The risk of loss
inhibits many empaths. Again, they are driven by the inner ideal that

they must be all accommodating and understanding; an ideal that can only lead to depletion and imbalance.

Here one can face the fear, speak the truth and put the cards on the table. She can write to him, sharing the truth and stating her new parameters. "I'm changing. I'm not who I was when you were a child and I'm no longer offering what I gave when you were a child. As adults we have to find a new way of relating." The risk does hold the possibility of anger and rejection, but that too may be aligned. It becomes very difficult to relate to and stay connected with people who only want the relationship from their perspective. Such people are often child-like; seemingly unable to place any limits on their own needs and wants unless the other person firmly holds the boundary. They often don't try to change because this child-like behavior is rewarding; they often get what they want from some people, especially empaths. Acknowledging the "what is" of the situation and being willing to act accordingly, as in setting limits and boundaries, creates the alignment that serves you best, and it may hold within it the opportunity for the other to grow as well.

Be willing to explore and consider your responses.
Be willing to revisit them and examine them.
Be willing to change your mind.

Empaths use understanding as a form of denial of their own needs and wants, especially so in a relationship. A client shared how she can feel into the situations in her life and find empath ways to balance them. She later said in an off-handed way, "I've sort of given up worrying about getting married. There seem to be so many reality-factors to deal with. We are together and I don't think it matters that we're not married." Perhaps this is a true statement, but it may also be a denial; leaping over her feelings and not exploring them in fear of facing conflict. Contrary to marriage not being essential for her, there may be something very important in the energy of being married and she seemed to resist even allowing that consideration.

Many people experience the energy of publicly, legally and sacredly bonding in marriage as different than living together. The ritual is iconic and holds a cultural energy of connection. An empath who seeks merging, community and bonding cannot just dismiss those pulls without exploration and examination. With a willingness to look at such feelings, you might find several options. If the external situation is really impossible, there could be a sacred ceremony instead of a legal one. The core issue here is to not leap over your feelings and take action without a full consideration. Even then, be willing to revisit and re-examine at another time earlier ideas and agreements.

Our client found the idea of re-opening the question of marriage disconcerting and an array of questions arose. Is another subconscious feeling being met by not examining her decision? Is some aspect of herself more comfortable with a sense of distance from her partner? Are there unrecognized elements that keep her from fully committing to her partner, creating a need to stay incomplete? Is she responding to an unexamined interpretation of what *he* needs and wants?

The concerns within such questions are most often connected to the fear that the other will not accept *all* of you. "Does he see me clearly? Am I willing to risk testing that he really does see me clearly and accepts me as I am?" When one is in relationship, there can be the pull to *modulate y*ourself; to want to reveal only the aspects you are comfortable with or even more so, what you think your partner is comfortable with. In a true, open marriage, one will eventually be exposed. Allowing consideration and inquiry into your fears is the way to open to another option and choice.

This couple did explore these questions and eventually married. She discovered an unexpected benefit. "Now that I am married, it seems to have settled something for my mother." Marriage was very symbolic to the mother and allowed an energetic separation from her daughter; a separation the daughter had desired for a long time. Through the symbol of marriage, the mother was now willing to see her daughter as settled and separate. "Mother made some kind of statement that "since I'm married she won't see as much of me." In this case, as the mother was quite elderly, this statement was also a hidden acknowledgement of her own evolving changes around separation. When you are willing to look for the truth in yourself, that willingness flows to those around you. Your own journey can serve as energetic models for others. Daughter looks for the truth of her moment and it opens and flows into Mother finding the truth of hers.

Use the principles of empath energy in relationship to discover and allow connection with another.

- Acknowledge to yourself the difference of your nature.

- Allow your idealizations to mature and reflect what is present.

- Discover and create new your own models of relating.

- Don't judge yourself and make limiting comparisons.

- Be willing to consciously examine your needs and desires, your fears and defenses.

- Be willing to live your life with passion and risk.

- Be willing to explore, examine and revisit your responses.

- Be willing to change your mind.

CHAPTER FIVE

DANCING WITH THE PHYSICAL

*The most important thing for an empath to do physically
is to let the energy flow and be expressed.*

Empaths are often challenged by how the physical body adapts to the flow of empath energy. There may be a history of life-long migraines and insomnia and other kinds of disturbances in the energy patterns, even when the body is healthy. As the body tries to adjust to different energies, anomalies and health conditions may arise.

Allow your energy to flow and be expressed, even if it is to yourself in a journal or sharing with your close friends. The principle is to let go of handling the energy or processing your emotions too quickly. Allow yourself to be with what you feel. Let go of leaping over the truth of your feelings. Be aware of your pull to feel comfortable mentally understanding a situation, rather than truly feeling it.

People often fear that allowing the *recognition* of energy or feeling will make it become an unchanging reality. "If I acknowledge that I am afraid, if I acknowledge that I am depressed – I will always be this way." Conversely, empaths are often afraid they *will* impact the energy and have consequences they did not anticipate. This fear may arise from the empath sense of realities where energy is moved and mutated by direct intent. Intent can impact and move energy in this present reality, but direct manifestation is mitigated against by form and the experience of linear time. Such fears lead to the desire to hide from the truth of your feelings and awareness.

> The body-mind-spirit system is not merged,
> but an interacting hybrid.
> Expressing your emotional energy
> reduces the impact on your body.

Energy moves and manifests indirectly and erratically because physical density impacts and affects the Web of Interconnection. If you are working in an *energetic* realm, the flow is only through energy. Linear time and physical density affect energy; moving, warping and shifting it. Energy that is *unexpressed* will find its own way to be expressed. This may be a smooth, flowing unconscious process. In some situations when energy is held in or unconsciously expressed through the body, the energy may solidify, creating changes which may eventually become physical or health-related problems. The interaction of the body-mind-spirit system leaves room for anomalies and events to occur in response to the myriad connections. Giving energy conscious expression sets up a smooth passage for releasing energy.

The model of psychology with its idea of "talking it out"
is such a prominent paradigm because it is an efficient tool
of letting conceptualized knowledge be expressed.

Verbal expression is often the simplest and most direct form of allowing energy to flow. It is a most efficient process because it engages the intellect in conscious understanding. Some people opt for physical expression alone – just letting the energy out. This can be a direct and effective approach, but reflection and a degree of comprehension are more integral and useful in the long run. When you just physically express the energy, the conceptual meaning held within the energy may never be acknowledged. The underlying meaning and other links and connections may continue to exist as unexpressed energy which can undermine the patterns in the physical body. Exclusively body-focused people may suddenly become ill and collapse, in spite of their seeming in optimal physical health. Unacknowledged energy tends to anchor itself within the body and may consistently impact the whole. Naturally, this is not always the case or the only reason for sudden illness or physical collapse, but unacknowledged and unexpressed energy can be contributing factors.

Talking it out and talking things through are useful and often powerful, but are not the *only* tools for working with emotions and energy. You often have to create a whole regimen geared toward moving energy which includes other elements of releasing energy, such as massage and body work, acupuncture, Tai Chi, etc. The idea is to allow an approach of complimentary and supportive tools as needed. You may keep one focus prominent at a time, but keep your attention open to seeing what else might be useful. The key to living a flourishing life is *movement;* movement of energy, ideas, interest, excitement, and so on.

Movement is an interactive dance with All There Is.

Movement does not necessarily mean linear progression. It is also the opposite of "getting it" and getting things settled. Rather, it is an interactive dance with All There Is. It is allowing and permitting yourself to flow with the rhythm, pulse and beat of energy that comes to you. Movement is a dance with the life energy that flows through you, often connecting you to what you know, as well as what you will come to know. It is a dance which can let you experience what you may never come to know through thought and concept alone. Movement is a dance that can be used just for free-flowing energy expression. Goals may be achieved through this flow, progression *may* occur, but the dance *itself* holds the primary meaning and purpose, not the goal. The Dance of Life, expressing the Interconnection of All Things, is part of the joy and vitality of being alive and present.

Inner patterns can be modulated, but it is often more useful to accommodate them.

Many empaths have sleep patterns that are atypical. They may have several days of less sleep and then one day of many hours of sleep. Or they may go strongly throughout the day and when they finally stop, fall asleep right where they are. You may be very active for four days and then just barely there for two. You may find that the end of the week is really hard and your energy feels depleted. You can modulate these patterns to an extent. It may be more useful to acknowledge the rhythm and need within the pattern and accommodate it. In doing so, the cycle or duration of the pattern is often accelerated and lessened. If in the past you felt drained and listless the whole weekend recovering from the previous week, you might remember to use Friday as your renewal night. By consciously accepting and acknowledging your need and requirements and setting your response in motion, you can activate patterns that support you.

> Paying attention to and acknowledging patterns
> can impact how long you need to stay in the pattern.

Physical ups and downs often mean you are ignoring or overriding signals as they occur. On its own, the body is very workman-like and directly efficient. It says, "Throw the circuit-breaker!" and your energy switches off because you weren't paying attention to the signal of tiredness. Bring your focus and attention more quickly to acknowledge your needs and requirements. In addition, you may physically collapse because you *judge* your needs. "How can a grown man possibly go to bed at 8:30?!" You make yourself stay up and do things, which you often end up having to do over because your concentration was impacted. You override your exhaustion and two days later you fall asleep at 7 PM in front of the television with your dinner on the coffee table. As you pay attention and acknowledge your patterns and the needs within them, you shorten their time-cycles and actually give yourself *more* time by qualifying what you will and will not do. Renewal time is essential for everyone and more so for empaths, who truly require "quality time."

Empaths consistently require time away from other people.

Even if you cannot be totally alone or separate in your environment, you need an *aspect* of your energy away from others. This occurs when you immerse yourself in another focus – a good book, a compelling film, art, crafts, crossword puzzles, knitting. Use what fully engages your focus and narrows external input to create a time and space where you can be unresponsive to the outside world.

Empaths may be less impacted by their pets, but sometimes you may need to put the cat out or not sleep with the dog or move the bird to another room. People who work with animals consistently require time completely away from the environment and the animals themselves, particularly if work involves animals who are sick or hurt.

**Allow yourself to listen, recognize and ask
what your own body-system requires.**

Consider that the body-system holds a level of awareness of what it requires. In acknowledging what you are drawn to, you may discover what serves you best. Certain characteristics show up regularly around empaths and the body. Typically there is a high requirement for dense protein. You may find at times you are a lapsed vegetarian because you really crave meat; often red meat. See if you can go with this new choice or find a substitute that really meets the craving. In addition, you may find that you must eat with regularity "3 square meals a day," and include dense vegetables like potatoes and carrots. These dense elements often serve as grounding and efficient fuel for what we call the velocity of the empath energy. Others may find that they are drawn to eat lighter and begin to eliminate foods they liked before. Still others find only particular foods or ways of preparing foods call to them. This fuel matches still another energy velocity. You may discover what was prominent and required for many years begins to change and you are called in entirely different directions.

Rather than approach what is needed in your diet primarily from an idea, principle or concept of health and well-being, allow yourself to listen and *recognize* what your own body-system requires. Allow yourself to *ask* what it requires. Be willing to listen and perhaps make changes that do not reflect your current ideas of health and wellness or more so, of your ideal self. Find the ways which feel integral and supportive, knowing they may change once again.

Certain supplements seem to be supportive and consistently required by empaths; particular the water-soluble vitamins – Vitamin C and the B-complex. Potassium and Magnesium are also supportive. Many empaths make good use of the energetic supplements such as Bach Flower Essences and other flower and gem essences. Homeopathic remedies are often useful for specific symptoms or situations.

Physical movement is very beneficial for
transmuting and transducing energy.

The key is to find what suits you, draws you, connects and resonates with you. Placing it in the context of moving energy through you, ask, "What will work best for me at this time?" You may get an idea that feels familiar or one you have enjoyed before. You may find yourself considering something you would never have tried or joining a friend or group in a new activity. You may find you simply enjoy walking more. See what arises in the context of *"energy movement"* – rather than ideals of health or "what's good for you."

The Energy Dance invites the body-mind
to allow energy to transform and flow
through unplanned movement.

The "Energy Dance" is unstructured movement designed to facilitate transmuting energy. You may be drawn to do this first thing in the morning or after work or even before bed. It's a most simple tool. Just turn on music, listen, *wait* and then begin to allow your body to move to the music *as it will*. You may flow into a "dance" or you may find that only small movements emerge, such as moving an arm, turning in a circle, bending to the side. The point here is not to dance as in a set idea of the mind, but to *invite* the body-mind to *allow* energy to flow, transform and move out of the body through movement. Allow the Energy Dance to continue until you find you simply come to a stop. The body will lead you with whatever timing occurs – one minute or five or ten. Rather than playing a CD, try just turning on a radio, which adds still another element of fluidity. By taking away direct control of the music, you are allowing and permitting what may come. Turn on the radio and allow the music to flow from the moment.

The Energy Song is another method of allowing energy to flow.

Picture this as a variation of singing in the shower. In fact, most people find the shower the perfect place for the Energy Song, but it is just as effective while walking in the park, being at home or whenever it arises. Again, the idea is not to sing a song, but to allow "song' to flow out. Begin by humming or toning. Close your eyes and let the sounds simply flow out. Often an Energy Song is more like toning than singing. If words form, allow them to flow. If you find yourself singing a song you know, just allow it. Like the Energy Dance, the song will have its own flow and will find its own completion. People report singing in tones, pitches or what seems like languages they do not recognize and that only come present on these occasions. One woman always finds she sings chants that sound similar to Native American songs. A man found he always sang in strong 'sounds' that were more like clicks and deep staccato tones. Others find lovely songs, complete with words and refrains, emerge.

Empaths report finding these routines refreshing in a unique way. They can serve as a clearing or cleansing of your energy system. Find the rhythm or routine that works for you, be it daily, every other day or once in awhile. Once a tool is present in the tool box of your consciousness, it is available and waiting for you.

> The important principle is to explore these tools
> and food and exercise regimens from the inside-out.

When something comes to your attention, stop, feel and ask, "Is this appropriate for me at this time?" Allow a response to arise and then stay with it awhile before you take action. Bring your conscious discernment into play as well. If you sense you would do well to take a higher daily dosage of Vitamin C, for example, read up on it; get more information on the internet, ask a practitioner. Make use of awareness tools, such as muscle testing or using a pendulum. Thoroughly check out what effects ideas may have on you. *Confirm* your sensings and then, using a full discernment, make a choice of action. Take a balanced action; try something in a small degree and gauge its effect.

> Flow and mutability are key aspects of the empath.

Change and ebb and flow in routines are to be expected. You may find some key requirements that seem to be ever consistent, but on the whole, be aware of noticing when change is required. Listen and look for clues. If you find you are forgetting to take your Vitamin C, inquire into why this routine has changed. Perhaps it is time to reduce the dosage or change your daily pattern of taking it. When you are working with items such as Flower Essences, come to them intuitively first. Literally choose the bottle you are drawn to and *then* read the meaning associated with that particular item. Use the information to focus your awareness on what underlying energy or issue may be at play.

Vitamin supplements can also reveal underlying stresses. Finding you are requiring higher doses of Vitamin C may indicate you are under stress and may need to put aside a project or take breaks more often. In addition, choose a food source of the vitamin you seem to crave or conversely, when you find you are drawn to drinking lots of citrus juice, consider adding a Vitamin C supplement. All these approaches remind you to engage in dialogue with your body and learn to trust and build upon that flow of awareness and knowledge.

> **Coping mechanisms that are very physical
> are more difficult to change because they are
> direct and efficient for the process of protection.**

A client shared that she used food as her balancing system. "It slows everything down and the image that came to me earlier was because I absorb a lot of energy from people, food and the fat soften the blows. I feel nice and soft now, but my body is starting to degenerate because of the weight and I know I need other coping mechanisms." Here she has recognized how on one level this pattern has been useful, and as we say "direct and workman-like" – the body will serve as insulation from the intensity of energy. On the other hand, she sees that the usefulness now has a higher cost to her.

Coping mechanisms that are anchored in the physical, like eating, are more difficult to change because they are very direct and in one way, efficient for the process of protection. Eating patterns are very common. You may simply gain weight because the body responds to the need for a filter and insulation. Thinking about yourself and what you do can set in motion the idea, "I want to try to change this. I am going to allow this change. I am going to change. I am changing."

Remember that the body is holding a sense of protecting you with insulation and filtering and that sense is infused with a lot of intense energy. To support change, you will want to engage that *protection* element. Connect with and engage in dialogue with the protection aspect. When you just declare, "I'm going to do this." and the body-mind says, "I don't feel safe enough," it simply will not move with your idea. The body-mind energy will override your mental contention and continue to try to do what *it* knows works. Understand that patterns you may want to change or that you feel are undesirable are usually rooted in that which feels effective and useful and known to other aspects of yourself.

Everyone carries their own paradoxes, opposing wants and needs. Aspects represent individual pieces that develop at different times and from varied events and causes. These aspects feel disconnected and separate and do not operate in an integrated way. They can have multiple, paradoxical agendas. Think of these feeling as voices wanting to be heard and felt. They are the children of your conditioning. When you can allow and accept that there may always be such pushing and pulling and disconnected compartments, you can see these separate aspects as emotional states that *interact* with the whole of you. Approaching change knowing you may have to dialogue with resistance supports allowing, inviting and *engaging* change. Engaged change acknowledges the loss of the familiar and seeks to find ways to address that which was met by the earlier pattern.

Honoring your need for a sense of protection,
you can apply your intent to transmute
physical protection patterns into *energetic* patterns.

When you recognize that food has been the effective tool for comfort and protection, and by acknowledging that inner concern, you can begin to consciously create a new supportive ritual recognizing the need for protection. With the important elements of recognition and acknowledgment included, a new pattern can evolve from earlier patterns and can eventually replace them. It is useful to link the emerging new attitudinal or energetic pattern to a correlating physical aspect. As an example, before you eat something for comfort, you could engage an energy movement symbolic of your intent to eat differently, such as turning in a spiral five times before you go to eat. Here the spiral holds the energy of transformation. Drinking a glass of water before eating can serve as a symbolic act. Reach for a glass of water before you reach for a comforting food as a way of interrupting the familiar pattern. Drink your water as a ritual, with the idea that "This is going to clear this pattern now negatively impacting me. Cleansing water helps me remember my new choice."

In addition, to honor the needs of the pattern, seek out alternatives and substitutes that really fulfill the need for comfort and protection, pleasure and delight. Symbols model your intention to create new patterns. Symbols hold the focus of your attention, which can assist in the development of new neuronal connections and pathways in the brain. The principle is to create personal symbols and rituals to help interrupt the known pattern and support another pattern to emerge.

Intentions are useful tools, but you must be willing to listen
and find the inner alignments and connections to them.
Be willing to revisit your feelings
and situations again and again.

When you are not successful in changing your patterns, it may be that you have not found the inner pathway to do so. Consider *yourself* as a web of interconnection; linked in ways you understand and in ways you do not. Invite awareness to come present. Truly ask, 'What can work for me?' and again, be willing to *not* explore the answer. Can you consider that some patterns may be shifted or changed in the moment or perhaps never? This is another aspect of being willing to release the outcome. Perhaps the change-action of your pattern simply is not yet aligned and is waiting, as it were, for the right time, the right option, the right information or support.

Being willing to release the outcome of intention
can actually expand the focus of your intent.
When you are open to another outcome,
something which may serve you more fully,
in ways you cannot yet see, can come present.

A client was working very hard to make some pattern changes. She shared, "I have been working with setting my intention, but it occurred to me to wonder about how my own intentions might negatively impact someone else or even limit myself."

Intentions may set a pattern in motion, but it is based on only what you can see and know in the present moment. Knowing this, you can

104

allow a fuller consideration by adding a balancing element to your intention, as in being willing to *release the outcome*. This simple phrase *expands* the focus of your intention energy and through that opening can allow something that resonates with *aspects* of your intention, but may serve you more fully in ways you did not imagine. Releasing the outcome does not ask you to give up the essence of your dreams and desires. It only asks you to let the specifics be more mutable and permeable. You may want a brand new car, but if a good used car with great mileage and a good price shows up – let yourself consider the option that presents itself. It may serve you better than your ideal.

Many people also add another caveat, as in "I hold this intention for my fullest good." Phrases such as this also acknowledge that what often seems the clear path, may in fact, *not* be what is most useful for the fullness of yourself. See *releasing the outcome* and *fullest good* as two expansive partners to help you let your egoic mind be more permeable by acknowledging there may be clearer alignments in the universe than those you can first desire or see.

A client shared that he feels he has a "higher self" that understands the origin of a health problem he was facing. He feels this greater part of him could know the resolution or the next step towards resolving the problem. He wondered how he can make greater use of such a capacity. This idea of asking and listening is a useful one. It may be more useful to consider your connection with the All as more expansive than the literal concept of higher self. Feel into and recognize your connection with the vastness and the true worldwide web of interconnection, where information exists and is accessible. Initiate the "Empath Google" by asking your questions and see what information flows to you.

> Post a query on the cosmic bulletin board.
> Let yourself be willing to not know and listen.
> Allow yourself to receive the information,
> however varied, different or challenging it may be.

Following the internet metaphor, you can easily flow from the empath Google to the cosmic bulletin board. To post your query, ask from your mind and heart, perhaps even speaking aloud. "I don't know what to do, so I am putting my question out to the Web. What do I need to look at here? What can help me?" Allow yourself to step away from what you already hold and know. One way to allow yourself to receive information which feels too different or challenging is to *separate* receiving from taking action. Receive and consider the information and then bring your tools of discernment and alignment into play. Just as a link on a web page can take you to a very different topic, information you receive from your own queries to the All may not be the direct or specific answer but in fact, may open a pathway of awareness which leads you to a very different place.

> It is essential and freeing to keep in mind that there
> Will always be areas of unknowing in your life.

It is not in the nature of reality that you can know all. Be open to exploring and learning. In the end, your only true option is to find the ways and means to simply be with that which does occur in your life, just as it is. All options flow from this base of acknowledgment. Acceptance of the actuality of your life is not a capitulation, but a willingness to see and acknowledge what is present. From there you can seek knowledge, awareness and action to impact, change, manage and be with your life as it is.

> **Tools of awareness are not promises**
> **that all will be resolved and balanced.**

Your willingness to be aware, and the tools you bring to that awareness, do not *guarantee* resolution, balance, safety, lack of pain or distress and a happy, peaceful life. You may find many ways to make your life easier and happier, but you cannot control life to match your ideals of happiness. If your ideals are the only focus or goal of awareness, eventually you will be disappointed.

See your awareness and the tools you use to focus your attention as openings or portals to recognize that you are part of All There Is *however* it manifests in your life. The All is equally present in every aspect of life – love and loss, birth and death; every pairing of opposites. You may not personally come to know the fullest meaning of why difficulty and strife is present, but you can find how to be present in the truth of the moment. Your connection to the All is available as strength and knowledge.

The energy of connection brings illumination in times of challenge and frustration and opens to the strength, endurance and power that becomes available in difficulty. You are never alone in your challenge. The music and flow of the All is always waiting for your attention and through that attention, it comes present. Let yourself find the spark of radiance always present– in joy and challenge, wherever you are in life.

Empaths are energetic and physical beings.
Make peace with your two different kinds of energy.
Make peace that you may not be wholly one or the other.
Make peace that some things you know energetically,
you cannot experience physically.
Discover the excitement of this dance of balancing,
rather than holding only to the frustration
of what you see as its limits.

CHAPTER SIX

CHILDREN and CHILDHOOD

*When you have a core of empathic nature,
it is a challenge to be with those who move
from a different, non-empathic energy.*

The quality of empathic connection is growing and many of you are bringing a new energy. You are precursors for capacities and abilities that are evolving and coming more present. Some of these qualities are being awakened. Other qualities can be seen expressing in young children coming into life with this energy. As you explore the nature of yourself and embrace your empath consciousness, you become true models of living with this awareness.

Although you may feel keenly aware of your different nature, eventually you come to learn the culture you are born into; how to operate within it and be part of it, even as if feels uncomfortable or constricting or rejecting. The inner strength of your empath nature is woven within what you learned and began to express emotionally as a child. Now you are moving toward an integral expression of the facets of your development. Empaths are dancers between realms, moving between two foundations of awareness and knowledge – empath nature and human nature anchored in your time and place.

Empath children often carry burdens of guilt about
the situations they were unable to move, rebalance or fix.

Empath children often struggle with expressing the unacknowledged shadows of their parents, or becoming the symbols of those shadows. They are often part of families where their empath qualities are not shared by or are dormant in other family members and the difference is challenging to the child. Often these children are in families where a parent is unable to connect with and express their own feelings. These parents struggle with an ongoing sense of disconnection and often evolve strong defenses against this feeling. They are then uncomfortable when they recognize the capacity of their empath child to connect with them and others. The child usually moves toward this parent, perhaps penetrating the parent's defenses, that paradoxically often causes those very defenses to become more rigid or dense.

Thus the parent/child relationship becomes one of push-pull, attraction and repulsion. In addition, the empath child is pulled to resolve and heal mother, father, sister, brother and all the family dynamics. The impossibility of this is not recognized by the child and they feel guilt, because they recognize a capacity to balance things and have not yet learned the *limits* of this capacity. Understanding that such patterns can exist is one step toward allowing yourself to acknowledge the deep impetus to bring balance and healing, and learn to separate your true self from this responsive child-self.

There is an image of a large family being a loving, intimate group, but parents in large families often do not respond intimately to a single child – they respond to "the children." The children themselves often relate primarily to the group and forge stronger bonds with certain siblings. Empath children in such situations often feel adrift. They see themselves as part of a *whole*, but here the whole does not respond intimately in a way that matches the empath child's desire and capacity for intimacy.

A client shared, "My friend and I could merge somehow. We could send mental messages. When we were together our minds were like one mind, two bodies. It was wonderfully playful and exuberant, but it became stifling when she wanted to control and direct it. I have always wanted this kind of connection." The experience of merged energy, flowing in and out of each other's energy, is more typically seen in children; the iconic "best friend" of childhood. Empath children may also find this kind of connection with animals or with "energetic" beings, usually understood as imaginary friends. But in this empath flow of connection, change can still be experienced as dissonance, with any separation being negative. You cannot cling to moments or ideals of happiness and connection. The ebb and flow of life is always in motion, requiring us to cultivate balancing. As you mature, culture sees such merged, flowing intimacy as more appropriate for love relationships, rather than friendships. Culturally, women are more supported in having an intimate, "best friend." Men often have to cloak their intimacy in activity, as in sports or clubs.

Many empaths are very defensive about their capacity to feel or sense what may not be readily seen by others because as children, this capacity was typically denied. This early denial creates a strong need to have your experience of reality confirmed or acknowledged in some degree by those you are intimate with. Recognizing that denial can support you in letting your defenses around this issue soften, and it can expand your willingness to share with those close to you. A less defended person can easily ask their friends and partners to support them with simply acknowledging, "Yes, you do get these senses."

> In a culture of empaths, a language
> and culture of receptivity would evolve.

What if you were raised in a culture where everyone was receptive and sensitive and such traits were acknowledged? The culture and its social norms would evolve from those perspectives. You could look at a child and say, "Oh are you sensing something, dear?" The child would close their eyes and say, "Yes, Mother, I feel Uncle Fred is really very sad and lonely." In such a culture it would be appropriate to follow through on this sensing and say, "Fred, the child had a sense about you. Is something going on with you?" And in the same way, Fred would be comfortable to receive this awareness and respond with, "Yes, I have been struggling with something," and further sharing could occur. A language and culture of receptivity would evolve. Empath children would develop in a society which naturally reflected and supported their innate capacities. In our society where a language and culture of receptivity has not fully evolved, you can create your own models of socialization to support the innate empath way of being; for yourself, for others and for the children.

Many empaths internalize the message that
sensing everything *is* their job and this is
often reinforced as part of their role in the family.

Empath children live in a world of many messages, often mixed and paradoxical. They are asked to be sensitive and receptive and at the same time, often suffer negative responses when they are so. "You should know that Mommy has a headache. And you should see that your sister is crying." The normal kinds of expectations of and constraints on children are increased in the empath child who really *can* tell that mother has a headache and is in pain and knows why sister is crying. Thus, typical super-ego development is amplified by the inner belief that "I have this capacity. I could be a healer, a psychic. I *should* do this." As an adult you can move toward rebalancing these inner messages by remembering that empath responsibility and accountability is anchored in striving to be clear with yourself. Clarity arises from knowing you cannot see everything and it is not your job to do so. In focusing on your responsibility to self-inquiry and asking questions about the situations you find yourself in, you will discover what actions are possible, for you to take, if any at all, and where the actual limits of your responsibility lie.

Empath children desire to heal and balance the family.

Empath children often feel they cannot leave home until all is well. As they grow older, the urge to have things be balanced grows stronger and the goal becomes "When they are all set, I can leave." When things cannot be balanced, the empath child often comes into some crisis or opportunity of their own, which gives them inner permission or forces them to move into the world. Often no one actually tells them they cannot make everything all right, because the family often wants to hold to the belief and possibility the child can indeed "heal" whatever is not in balance.

You learn many ways of interaction within the family. The fortunate child quickly realizes what mountains cannot be moved, which people are not impacted by their feelings or cries. When this is *not* learned, years of unexpressed frustration and anger are held within. You can see this clearly with people who always rail against that which cannot be changed. They did not learn the discernment involved in recognizing that there are places in life where one cannot be the change-agent. Many hold on dearly to the feeling that explaining and understanding any situation will bring a shift. They have difficulty in recognizing that others have learned to use the energy of anger or confrontation around change and may have no interest in or capacity to respond to explanations and understanding.

Many empaths carry a deep fear that techniques are manipulation, asking you to change yourself into a false person.
The wounding in relation to technique is from the earliest years.

In a workshop after a session focusing on techniques for managing receptivity, a participant was almost moved to tears. "I've really struggled today. I feel disconnected. Suddenly it feels that all these techniques are just *manipulation*. I'm longing to be in that place of connection and I'm not and I don't want to manipulate to make something happen. I don't want to reject where I actually am in the moment. So I am sharing now that I feel this way. I often use a comparison of states and experiences to judge myself and forget to simply be fully where I am." Many empaths share this underlying concern that technique is manipulation, rather than a way to manage or balance aspects within situations. This feeling is further reinforced because techniques can indeed be used to manipulate.

Many children are affected by the requirements of parents and culture. Empath children in particular experience required systems, prescriptions and techniques as a wounding because these cultural requirements often ask them to deny or relinquish essential aspects of themselves. Empath children learn to change themselves from the earliest years. Many children are actually *asked*, in one way or another, to *be* the empath child and are then punished for it. You are wanted to be a sensitive, responsive child; to be the child who always comes when Mother is upset. But, when the empath child is overwhelmed with it or declares that mother is upset not because she has a headache, but because she hates Father, the child is rejected or punished harshly for it. The child is told again and again, in so many ways, "Don't be like that. Control yourself. Don't cry. Don't be so emotional!" And so what do dear empath children do? They try giving their parents what is wanted. "I won't cry. I won't be emotional. I'll be how they want me to be." The wounding is not only that you are asked to manipulate yourself into a false person, but you are also required to learn how to manipulate the truth of what you know. Empath children learn how to couch what they sense and feel in an acceptable way to have any chance of being heard. They can't share their senses or feelings, except in convoluted, hidden ways.

The experience of most empath children is
that how they *are* is rejected.
They are made to feel inherently wrong and told
their behavior does not fit the customary models.
This deep rejection is carried in adulthood.

The experience of innate wrongness is built upon a litany of parental and social commands. "Get over those emotions. Handle those emotions. Stop those emotions. You shouldn't have those emotions. You are too emotional." This experience is confounded by the fact that many people are uncomfortable with the empaths' degree of intensity. Recognizing this fact yourself means you do not have to accept and *internalize* their reactions as true assessments of you. In acknowledging the other's feeling you can simply say, "Yes, I *am* very emotional and I see it is too much for *you*. I can understand that."

A workshop participant declared, "When I think of myself as an empath, I talk about us as being aliens on the planet. Recognizing we are empaths and sharing about it is "standing up" for each other." She shared her unique articulation about her need to find a model of being that matched her sense of self. "Empaths are from Arcturus and somehow the stork got lost and we feel like strangers in a strange land. I've noticed that a lot of us Aliens incarnate into families where we can learn how to be an Earth-person. This works until we come to a point in our life when we have to stop playing the role and we have to stand up and be counted. It's like we're in an auditorium, where someone says, "All aliens please stand up." And we wait for that first person to stand up, so I can stand up too. I feel we need people to stand up and be counted in terms of their Alien-ness. Recognizing we are empaths and sharing about it is "standing up" for each other. I can really get caught up in playing the role and losing sight that I am of a different nature. I have felt disconnected from myself and out of touch with my feelings. The hard part is discovering what do I really feel." This is a clear example of finding personal imagery that crystallizes the essence of her difference and gives her a way to consider herself. As in all symbols of identity, alien, empath, etc., you must remember to wear them lightly or the very models that help you understand yourself will become a constraint, limiting your understanding.

Empaths often internalize the unmet expectations of others and learn family roles that do not reflect the true nature of the child.

This is especially true in the early family environment. Empath children also internalize the displaced anger or frustration which is often aimed at them, particularly when they are trying to bring about resolution or compromise. In these situations, the empath child gets strong mixed-messages when others desire them to help the situation and resent the help or want to reject being helped or just turn the anger onto the child who hasn't been able to help.. At other times, the empath child deeply wants to help and has not yet learned that there are times they cannot help or help is not desired. Here, other family members may be angry with them for "interfering" or "getting in the middle" of things. The empath child usually does not understand the source of such responses and simply absorbs the angry feelings.

A woman who had been a quiet participant in the same workshop, finally spoke with great emotion. "I've been sitting here looking back at my own childhood and wondering how the brother I felt closest to couldn't see or feel the same things I did see, even though he was there with me. I didn't relate to any of my other siblings. Two siblings were twins and they shared a special relationship that I felt excluded from. I see the family role I chose was one of great difficulty; being a model soldier and living up to the expectations of being this strong person. When you have so much inside of you that you don't know how to express and you carry all the expectations of living up to being perfect – this perfect woman, this perfect soldier, this perfect daughter, this perfect person. It's overwhelming. I break down and begin to ask myself who I really am."

She gave herself a gift in the very breaking down she reports. She has been soldiering on all these years and now senses that perhaps she has "stayed too long at the fair." Many empaths do this; giving the situation or others a second chance, now a third. This response is led by the empath capacity to sense someone's *potential* and their feeling they can or *should* support that potential. Discernment is again the required principle. Potential may be there, but the aware empath must learn to ask, "Is this person I'm supporting connecting to their own potential? In this moment, am I the one who can help them?" Such questions can bring you to recognize more readily when the true answer is that you cannot help. Allowing discernment through inquiry supports your journey away from living only your "assigned" and familiar role and interrupts continuing to recreate your early role.

It is typical for an empath child to be
the odd-one-out member in a family.

The empath child accepts this distance from the family because it feels congruent with their own sense that they are somehow different. Typically, though, there is one parent, grandparent, aunt or family friend, who is simpatico to the child. They know you're different and accept it, even if they don't really understand you. The honoring of your difference is powerful because it creates a place of acceptable difference. Empath children often have mutable, ebb and flow connections with their siblings. It is particularly difficult for an empath child with siblings who are twins, since twins share an empathic bond that only extends to them and is exclusionary. The little empath wants to bond and merge and recognizes her siblings share it, but sees she cannot be part of it in the same way and the sense of being outside is increased.

Developmentally, all children share elements of mutability. The primary task in every child's life is to learn to make the world concrete through image, language and concept, reflecting the culture one is embedded in. The empath child strongly retains their sense and experience of *fluidity*; seeing and sensing in their own way. Often siblings and other children find this quality confusing, disconcerting and off-putting as they themselves are focusing on making the world more solid and less changeable. Most children accommodate their empath sibling with movement -- approach and avoidance, closeness and distance. Bonds are formed regardless of the difference, with siblings often serving as strong protectors for the empath from parents and the outside world.

> The empath sense of the capacity to be part of
> a collective is embedded in the Empath DNA.

One client expressed her recognition of this connection by sharing that when she considered doing what she wanted, she found herself automatically judging her want with the idea that wanting is taking from the collective itself. She feels inhibited and constricted about her own needs. Here is a reflection of an empath child's understanding of the whole and how that understanding is incomplete. You may sense a resonance of your sense of an empath collective, but that specific collective wholeness does not exist or flow in this reality of individuation. Empaths must learn the discernment of balanced wanting -- recognizing your own needs and desires. Allow them to be seen and considered openly and neutrally, without preconceived judgment. Learn to see your wants as not necessarily secondary to others. In neutral language, wanting is the clarity of what attracts your energy. This does not mean that every want is satisfied in a concrete manner, but all can be considered. Denying what has attracted your energy causes its own imbalance. Clear actions flow from learning discernment of what attracts or repels you and what feels neutral.

> To support an empath child, begin with the understanding
> that they are indeed sensitive and highly receptive.

A father shared concern about his five and a half year old son, whom we shall call Jason. The father was in the midst of a big career move.

The family had relocated away from family and friends, and the father often had to travel for weeks at a time in his new job. He was concerned that Jason was becoming more sensitive and reactive to the situation and he didn't know how to make it easier on the boy, as well as the rest of the family. Young Jason's story is a good example of approaches to support an empath child. Follow the dialogue as if you are the father asking for support.

When you want to support an empath child, begin by acknowledging to yourself and your son his sensitivity and receptivity. Support him in this fact of his nature and confirm to him that he is accepted and understood. Don't tell him that he is "too sensitive" or allow others to admonish him. Understand that Jason picks up unspoken emotions; feeling the undercurrents and unexpressed energy in the household. When he seems shy or overwhelmed, too cautious or frightened, consider this may be *exactly* his experience, no matter what the situation looks like to others. When Jason doesn't want to go into a new situation, maybe he is accurately picking up that the teacher is angry or there is something going on. Give him options, unless it is essential to do otherwise. Don't require him to "push through" his feelings; acknowledge his sensitivity. Give him permission to be himself in the moment. You can then help Jason learn tools to deal with his sensitivity. "Son, are you feeling you don't want to go there right now? Okay, we can wait a minute. Do you want me to do something to help you feel safer?"

It is deeply supportive for parents to share the truth with the empath child.

Most children, but especially empath children, are responsive to and comfortable with the truth of a situation. When things are going on, tell him. Jason senses it all and will feel your troubled energy is connected to *him*. You don't have to share all the details, just let him know something is going on with you. You can acknowledge that you know he feels your energy, "Yes Jason, you can tell Daddy is thinking about something, but it's about work, so don't worry about it."

It is so important to not give emotional responsibilities to empath children.

Don't tell Jason that he is responsible for his younger siblings. Don't tell him he is in charge, that he is the Daddy when you are away. He will *literally* try to take on this responsibility and he should not be responsible. He so strongly responds to others; putting their feelings first, not feeling his own needs or limits. As is often the case, his siblings are less sensitive than he is. They have a kind of self-centered strength he does not have and they do not need his protection.

Jason is especially sensitive to his mother, feeling all her unexpressed energy around the situation with his father and the move. His closeness with her also contains an element of fear. He is concerned that he is the cause of her anger and her "spiraling out" in this very difficult time and situation. It is clear and understandable to Jason that Father gets angry with things Jason may do, at his actions. But, Jason feels that Mother seems to get angry at *him*, at his very presence. He wonders if she is mad at all of them. He senses this strongly and feels that the flaw is in him. He does not have a clear enough picture of how change and stress can make people act angry and frustrated at another person, instead of what they are really upset about. Talk to him and give him the clear view. He cannot understand this on his own. Let him know that Mother gets angry at other things and then *reacts* to him. When Jason says "Mommy scares me." consider that there may be *something* about Mommy's energy that does scare him, even if she has not acted upon it. As Jason's concerned father, encourage Mother to appropriately express her feelings to you or another adult, and not deflect them onto the child. Don't let Jason take on the responsibility Mother's emotions. Ask her to join you in making it clear that what is occurring is not his fault.

> It is vital to not force empath children into
> cultural roles and models that do not reflect them.

Do not require Jason to be the "big brother" or the eldest, or to act like boys should. Support him in being him. See who he is. Help him be himself. Look at the principles of being an empath and see how it can apply to a child. Most adults have to *unlearn* the limits they took on to be like others; the pain they took on, feeling it was theirs. They have to unlearn the embedded belief that they alone were the cause of all effects to themselves and others in their childhoods. This is a common theme for most children, but it is more intense and exacerbated for the empath child. By addressing such understandings and beliefs with your child now, you can help him grow freer of such inner constraints.

Honor and acknowledge a child's receptivity.

Children rather accurately express what adults are feeling -- often emotions the adults have yet to acknowledge. Listen when children tell you what they feel and see, even if it seems inaccurate or has not actually occurred. Allow empath children to *not* like people or to not want to be with certain people. Never force connection on them. Give them permission to step away from a challenging situation. This is the most effective strategy for young empaths. Consider they may be *literally* picking up energy that is disturbing to them. When they have trouble sleeping at night or are afraid of the dark, again consider they sense something which upsets them. Acknowledge that they may feel things you do not share or understand or are not clear to you. Tell them that you will be there for them, help them learn about what they feel and sense. Create a caring, accepting, assuring structure or routine that makes them feel safe, and comfortable as they go to bed.

The child who is allowed to be receptive can then be supported in learning when and how to share or not to share.

A child who is supported in being sensitive can easily learn to balance sharing their feelings with the best friend or parent, but not with everyone. Expand your ideas about how children should be and support them in finding ways to be at home with their difference. Perhaps in this way, they can learn two languages as they grow -- Earth and Empath -- rather than having to go through the pain of unlearning limiting patterns and softening defenses. Perhaps their defenses can evolve more as attitudes of awareness, with skills and tools of balance. They can learn to apply versions of the empath tools and techniques.

The empath child will not find a world that is anywhere close to 100% aligned to their way of being. They *can* learn discernment about how they participate in the world. This is not lying or being untrue to oneself. Rather, it allows full awareness of the "what is" of the world, rather than seeking idealistic realities that are not available.

With awareness, you can raise children with spiritual maturity, for the parents as well as the child.

Empath children readily understand the nuances of sensing and feeling people and situations. They will not feel compromised or manipulated by recognizing boundaries or the need to use discernment. They will truly feel into these very things. They will come to understand that people must hear and learn in their own way. Their sensitivity will allow them to be comfortable in not telling Grandmom that the real reason she can't go up the stairs the way she did before is that she has grown larger or telling Uncle John that he has headaches because he is sad and misses Aunt Jean who died awhile ago. The strategies of life and communication make perfect sense to these sensitive children when you begin by acknowledging and allowing their sensitivity.

Use insight into how your childhood impacted you to support the sensitive empath children in your life.

All children come into life with the expectations and hopes of the family. The empath child strives to bring wholeness, joy, harmony and balance to the family. They often bring a calming element to conflicts in the family. Reflect upon your own childhood. This early role can continue throughout life and at times, this does flow as your true nature. At other times, you may feel *compelled* and *bound* by your own capacity to fulfill this role. Your astute sensitivity can become burdensome to, or even resented by, others. Understanding these elements helps create a supportive model for empaths to see more clearly and broadly. You can help others when you deepen your understanding of what has been embedded within you, seeing how this impacts the choices you make. Some choices are expansive, while others are contracted. Open to the possibility of new choices, led by clearer motivation. In this way, you can stand up for others, declare your nature, and reach out to the smallest among you.

Most adults have to unlearn the limits
they took on to be like others –
the pain they took on, feeling it was theirs,
or the burden they carry believing they were the
cause of all manner of difficulties in their childhood.
This is a common theme for most children,
but it is more intense and exacerbated
for the empath child.

CHAPTER SEVEN

SHARING THROUGH
QUESTIONS and ANSWERS

We all speak to each other and for each other.

The material in this book is the result of the queries, sharing, insights, and knowledge of the many individuals who participated in the workshops, lectures and personal sessions exploring empath energy. Awareness and knowledge are living energies evolving, growing and expanding in each exchange, interaction and connection.

A true demonstration of living within a connected collective is experienced when people join together with a willingness to listen; to share personal experiences and being willing to expose themselves to what they do not yet know. They look at facets yet to be explored and examine what is now ready to be seen. New doorways open and the familiar reveals a new aspect. They stimulate each other and refine articulations together. Touching into the collective supports individuals to bring new attention and awareness to their individual lives. This sharing is an integral aspect of this book with the many personal questions generously shared in the spirit of connection.

> Participants share recognition of a spiritual aspect to life
> and have chosen to consciously explore their spirituality.

Recognition of a spiritual aspect of life is the thread that binds the collective that forms in every workshop, lecture or personal session. Along with this, people have resonated with this articulation of empath energy and have joined in this exploration. Despite this core consistency, participants include all ages and come from varied economic and social strata, with varied backgrounds and interests.

Throughout this book, individual questions have been included within the context of each chapter. Following are mini-profiles of some participants; names and details have been changed for confidentiality. The question and answer dialogue is presented in a free-flowing manner. Perhaps you will resonate with those to who speak.

ళళళళళళళ

Ken first met us in his 40"s, having had spiritual awareness as a primary focus in his life for many years. His work life has been focused in computers, communications, writing and editing. Exploring the empath concepts supported him in more fully understanding his receptivity.

"Instead of just learning to cope with empath nature, can this capacity itself serve as a tool to help cope with life?"

Most people first come to the idea of the empath by having to find ways to cope with the overwhelming aspects of it. They have to cope with "I receive so much that I don't know what to do with it." Ken reminds us each to ask what *else* can happen with this capacity? Here is where you can enter into delightful exploration. The most common thing that people find is, of course, the capacity to be emotionally there for others. Not too surprisingly, in Western culture lots of empaths often end up either in helping professions or as individuals who are known for their empathy and caring -- be it at the office or the fire station or the bookstore. This isn't only a magnanimous giving, because there is the flow of energy the empath really loves -- the taste and feel, the vitality and exchange of it.

ஃ ஃ ஃ ஃ ஃ ஃ ஃ

Janine grew up abroad as a child of an officer on a naval base, keenly aware of her sense of difference. Perhaps these early experiences are the key to her life-long interest in a spiritually-focused life. She joined groups, followed a teacher and now lives a self-integrated spiritual life. She works in human resources for a large corporation.

"Working and thinking about empath energy, being positive and learning how to use it, I've had an encounter with someone that was troubling. In the end when they walked away I said, "What just happened here?" I had just met this person and we began a conversation and after a time, I felt something wasn't right. There seemed to be a hidden agenda and it felt massive and almost dangerous. I can only define my experience as being manipulated in a way I'm not totally clear about. What happened here, what did the person actually have to gain?"

129

Empath energy is immensely attractive and unfortunately it sometimes attracts people you are not drawn to yourself. Not only do these people recognize that your energy is open and receptive, they often find you actually understand them. At first you do not notice how different, odd or even disturbing their energy is, as your empath attention is focused on listening and moving to change, translate or transmute the energy. You have naturally and unconsciously moved into empath mode. Then, as in this case, you begin to sense the dissonance. Perhaps you realized you could not impact or mitigate this energy. Perhaps you realized this person is not actually relating to you, but only to the part of you willing to respond to them. This is why developing discernment is so vitally important for the empath. The dance of energy is embedded with your right and responsibility to yourself to stop dancing, close the door and leave the room. An empath must remember that because you *can* understand, can be responsive and can extend this energy -- it does *not* mean you *must*. You have to take care of yourself first. You have the right and responsibility to yourself to simply say "No, not now, no more," or even more bluntly, "Go away."

When boundaries and limits feel difficult and challenging, pause and consider that it is the empath impetus resisting the limit, rather than judging the boundary itself as wrong. Your task is to see into the truth of the present situation and use the balance of your discernment and awareness to modify your first impulse appropriately. It is not useful to hold a false ideal of being all-giving as it does not reflect the reality of life. Live in the world *as it is*, not as you want it to be.

*C*harlene is an artist, a lover of animals, especially horses. Her husband is a professor who has not shared her spiritual interests directly, but has been supportive of her endeavors. She has always had a few friends who share her interest in the spiritual perspective.

"I find many people resist me because I am different and I have trouble when friends leave me because of this difference. I feel as if I've gone through life with one group of people and then another group and still another, with no continuum. Why do I have this longing for continuum? Why can't I simply accept one group and then another as my norm?"

There are certain people in your life who *are* simpatico with you. Sometimes it is a sense arising in a moment of meeting, even if there is not duration to the continuum. This longing is common to most people. You know you are part of a Whole and want to experience that reflected in your reality. This knowing is amplified for the empath, who may carry an even deeper recognition of realities where cultures are unified, merged and sharing of the world is through energetic connection.

Empaths are often challenged in friendship and it is rooted in their capacity to dance between the worlds. They often sense more than what is currently present or what others might not see. They move toward finding what works for everyone, for the collective energy. But "between worlds" often means connections that flow in one place may not flow as easily in another. Your mystic friend may not feel comfortable in your conventional work-a-day world. Your family may not feel comfortable in your meditation world. You may be required at one time or another to modulate your environment; to be comfortable with a degree of separation in your world. You may need to soften your language with one group, but find you can flow more freely with another. There is no problem with this dancing if you consider it just another expression of the seeming paradox of life. When you let go of the expectation that there must be only a single flow or way to express your being, you can be at ease with the diverse flows that occur in life.

"I am thinking of studying a healing energy system, but I am concerned that this will be uncomfortable and too "out there" for my husband. He would certainly want me to do what I needed or wanted to do. I only need to be clear to him about what I want, but I am finding that hard to get to."

You are inhibited by your desire to be sure of his response and acceptance before you decide what you want to do. You are more concerned about putting *him* in an awkward place than discerning what may be essential to you. Allow yourself the possibility of considering what you want and need unfettered by your responsiveness to others as your primary focus. Consider that you have a right and responsibility to yourself to evaluate what may be important to you alone. Once you become clear, you can then place your caring for others into your consideration and from this whole, the course of action will emerge. By separating consideration from action, you allow yourself a freer inner journey.

"I was trying to decide if I should intervene and take action about a situation within a group I belong to. I had a meditation in which I was sitting in the light and the dark. I felt I was sitting in paradox. It was as if I were on a knife edge with my left side in the dark and my right side in the light. I tried to move over into the light, but the harder I tried, the more I seemed to end up in the dark. When I just let go and *allowed*, I was able to sit between the two. I found some reflective light there that went into the dark that way. I took this to mean to not take any action on the situation. The message seemed that allowing is the best way to bring light to a problem."

The real challenge in allowing is that there is not a *single* approach and allowing does not necessarily mean that you take no action. One of the paradoxes of allowing and permitting is recognizing the *vitality* within. Allowing is not a passive acceptance. Allowing and permitting does not abandon discernment or declare everything as perfectly fine as it is or mean that action is never required. There are times when allowing the truth of a situation asks you to be indignant and speak out and make a challenge or correction. At other times, it is more aligned to take no action. Again, discernment is the key.

In the most expansive understanding of being, everything may be in accord. Despite that further fullness, you are asked in your conscious life to take action, to bring energy, shift energy and interact with life. In each situation ask, "What can best serve here now?" Sometimes there is the gut reaction to speak up. Other times you might find, "No, now is not a time to speak." And at still another time the message is, "Not your action to take. Let it go." There are times when speaking up can help shift a situation. There are other times when people must simply experience a difficulty and find their own resolution. There may be times with no direct resolution or when you are not the one who can impact the situation. Techniques of allowing and permitting, of rapport and listening are not all mental decisions. They are attitudes that activate your deeper knowing through your capacity to tune in, touch in and access the whole movement of interconnection.

Consider another element to the meaning within the meditation. You translated the images of light and dark as in *opposition*. "Dark" can also represent receptivity, introspection, and quiet, lack of outside stimulation, interior worlds, labyrinth, space, other universes, and other realities. "Light" can represent activity, energy, focus, brilliance that dazzles the eyes or holds your focus and attention. The meditation may echo reaching the limits of your *perception* about what is "good and bad" action. Sitting in paradox is a reminder that these two aspects *intermingle* and exchange, and as in paradox, exist at the same time. Opening to energy allows aligned movement to come present.

"I find I am not able to bring any comfort at all to my 85 year old mother-in-law who lives in a nursing home."

Here is another example of opening to what you can or cannot do in a situation. Sometimes when one realizes that life is coming to its natural close, it is quite difficult to acknowledge and accept it. Often people have to go through great pain and suffering to leave life. They have to feel the energy that life has been *taken* from them before they

134

can open the door and go through it. They can't just "pass over" in the gentle manner you sense is possible. Your mother-in-law may feel she would like to give up the fight and easily let go, but giving up is not acceptable to her code of living. She does not value or respect the seemingly easy way. She will continue to resist taking pain medication and will continue to fight her decline. Your ideas of "letting go and going on" simply do not fit her world view. Part of her is frightened that she is weary of life and would like to let go and what you share upsets her because she feels you have seen her secret. People often use depression as a way to begin the separation. The ebb of energy makes it more permissible to go.

What is available to you is an opportunity to offer comfort and support at distance. Trust what can be used will be, and offer your caring energy without a need for acknowledgment or a tangible result. You may also find it useful to acknowledge to her a life fully lived; sharing her areas of accomplishment and completion -- life as a "job well done" -- rather than emphasizing moving on. Acknowledging the 'what was' can allow people to come to an acceptance of completion. Still another way to share with her is by "speaking on the wind." Hold her in your inner vision and share all your heart wishes for her. Speak the truth of your heart, including your own fears and senses. Release the energy of these words and allow that they can be used. Let the All discern how she uses the energy.

ૐૐૐૐૐૐૐ

Alison is a massage therapist who has studied many different energetic modalities and integrated them into her work.

"I feel very merged with my clients. At times I can feel changes within them and at other times it feels as if they are resisting change and growth. They need to take many steps when it seems to me they could take a leap. I try to simply hold the space for them, but I wonder how I can help them more definitely?"

Looking toward a definite outcome or trying to create a result is *not* your responsibility as either a therapist or an empath. What you *have* chosen to be responsible for is your willingness to share your ability. You've recognized a capacity within yourself which you offer to others, enhanced by sharing with integrity, accountability and balance. This offer is your true responsibility. Your private practice is the structure you created by which people can recognize your energy and skills and decide if they want to work with you. You offer physical relief to the body and emotional guidance as well, but you must be willing to release your expectations of the outcomes. What people take from life is their own responsibility and they have the right to accept or deny what is offered. Additionally, no one allows change unless they move toward it on their own. You cannot always know why people have to do things incrementally; why people have to return to an old pattern or cannot accept what seems a wonderful opportunity for growth. It may not be for you to know. Rather, it is for you to respect the other's path. You can offer the way you see, but you must honor their choices and needs. Consider that there are alignments in their choices, not only what you see as resistance, limitation or fear.

If a client continues to return, you will have opportunities to share what you see once again. On the other hand, if you have a client you find frustrating to work with, you have the right to not continue the client relationship. Allow yourself to consider if the relationship is aligned or not for *you*. You may say to yourself, "I find it very hard to work with people who cannot do the work in the same way as I do. I can, but find it uncomfortable, draining and very sad." You have the right to not be available when those people call or refer them to someone you feel might be more aligned with them. Once again, because you have a capacity and ability does *not* mean you have a cosmic mantle of responsibility to extend it to anyone who asks of it. Over-arching all is *alignment*. You have the right, no matter whatever you feel is flowing through you as an empath, to work with people you feel aligned to and it is your responsibility to discern this alignment. You are not a cosmic clinic that has to take anyone who comes to the door. You have the right to use discernment in your clientele. By operating with the fullest awareness for yourself, you can be available in the fullest way for others.

"Does a healer have to suffer physical ills or must a counselor have struggled with psychological ills to support another? People in my meditation group pronounce this as if it is undeniable fact."

The primary responsibility of a healer or counselor is to hold space for someone to explore and express themselves. This is linked with the counselor's capacity to listen, understand, share insight and awareness and is amplified by their willingness to transmute the energy they may receive. In that transmutation, a healer allows the energy to flow through with the fullest responsibility to release the outcome. Further, it is the counselor's responsibility is to maintain their *own* balance, wellness and health in order to be available in a balanced way. It is *not* their responsibility to take on or absorb another person's situation, pain or dilemma. Doing so is being seduced by the idea that *they* are doing the work; that they are healing the other. Healers, counselors and the like must be responsible to their own balance by eating properly, resting, and so on. They must hold a conscious intent that the energy is transmuted and released. Healers are *facilitators*. You come together, share energy and move energy together in ways you recognize and in ways guided by the interconnection of all things.

"I had a negative experience with a teacher of energy. The teaching was very hierarchal and expensive and at the same time, touted as channeling universal energy. In this kind of work I usually say I am not the source but merely the channel, but I feel I am still not clear about how to see myself in such work."

Saying "merely the channel" does reflect that you are not the source of the energy, but still reinforces the idea of the "Master Teacher" paradigm. In the idea of Unity consciousness, *inherent* equality is *recognized*. From this perspective one may have degrees of expertise and experience that can be taught, but mastery of knowledge is never held as that of a master over another. In this way, think of your willingness to channel energy as, "I am willing to recognize my interest in and perhaps my ability in being a receptive facilitator of energy." You consider and acknowledge your own capacity -- offering it as of value, but not elevating your position or ability. You do not need to approach the universe in the energy of the naive or novice. It is true that you can be without specific knowledge, but that does not limit you to operating only from a lesser position. When you come to learn or share yourself, you must get in touch with a sense of self-respect. Recognize your *own* willingness to work in integrity, with balance, thoughtfulness and respect. You can offer a willingness to give, aligned with your willingness to be responsible to how you give and further, be responsible to what may come from your giving and to what may seem to *not* come from what you offer.

Recognize a sense of authority about yourself and see this as *authorship*, as in, "I am the author, the maker, the creator of my actions and choices." This sense of authorship is imbued with the willingness to see and recognize truth and to be responsible and accountable to it. When you are learning, bring your focus primarily to the *principles* within the teaching. Techniques are useful and effective, but discovering and integrating the principles will support you in discovering your *own* techniques, approaches and applications. Open your perspective and allow evolving Unity consciousness to express through you and lead to broader understandings and models. How you live and explore life adds that very energy to the Whole.

"My mother and sister seem perceptive but they didn't pursue being an empath like I did. I often feel that my health condition, that they did not share, helped create or enabled my empath abilities."

The idea that you would need to have a condition to be able to touch into empath abilities is not accurate. Rather, it is possible that the energy of these capacities can make use of such situations. Challenges and anomalies can open to other abilities. A problem often turns people in a direction they might not have discovered as readily or at all. Energy pays attention to what is present rather than creating situations to facilitate growth. There are occasions where individuals have differences that are reflections of what you might call "energetic anomalies," as if the body accommodated the difference in a specific way, but these are rare and not typical.

ॐॐॐॐॐॐॐ

Kathleen is in her sixties. She has adult children, was born in another country, speaks several languages and works as an administrator in a large organization.

"After 9/11 for a short time people were friendly and connected to each other, but that didn't last very long. How come we can't keep the sense of connection?"

The all of "why" is unknown, but there are many different lines of connections and development. There is *consistency* in life, but not constancy. People often grieve this lack of constancy and the movement of change. Allow yourself to question the *model* of constancy. Question the ideal that life would be best if everything would stay constant in one energy or another. Consistency builds strong roots and a more flexible platform than that which is constant.

See consistency as the natural reflection of the movement of ebb and flow, serving as a supportive structure for the movement of the All. The crisis moments of life break through all the usual and customary patterns, allowing you to experience connection directly. In those moments, individuals move away from the divisiveness and separation typical in life and find a connecting flow from within shared crisis. When the crisis begins to shift, the intensity of the connecting thread lessens and the dominant pattern of separation returns.

People recognize and connect with the principle of Unity – the innate and immutable interconnection of all things. One hears "Unity" and may feel it as connection, as "all is one." What you forget is someone else may find the idea of such unity and connection as impinging upon them. "No. I don't want to be like him. I'm not a person like her. I'm not one of them." Here, their identification is anchored in how they are *different* from others, not how they are the same. That paradigm is much more prominent than the sensing of Unity. Accept and appreciate the times when connection arises, while acknowledging the reality that connection changes.

Unity and the connection that flows from it do not mean that life will always be easy, happy and smiling. Rather, Unity is what is available to you through the worst times of your life. Spiritual awareness and recognition of the All serve as a support, not as a formula for a nice life. There will be times that you will have absolutely no control over life. Events *will* happen to you. And it is in this very place that your awareness can bring you the energy of the All to support you. This expansive energy supports you in bearing and coping with challenge, in opening to options and choices and finding ways to move through or if possible, change the current situation.

"I think about being more open, but in my life there are a lot of people I feel are invasive. I was brought up to help them no matter what, but I have seen this is not always the answer."

Openness to life does not mean being open to and allowing everything that wants to come in. Openness to others is caring and useful, but it does not and cannot mean openness "upon demand" is required or even supportive. Allow your concepts to become more complex so you can hold a broader model of openness and helping, i.e., a model that has more options and choices of attitude and actions. You need to be cautious with the model of "openness is good – closed is bad." Being willing to be *emotionally* open, asks you to be willing to use discernment about the appropriateness of the *actions* you may take in response. You can be open to others and at the very same time be appropriately closed to taking the action others may want of you.

"What can you say around the connection that happens in the middle of divisiveness?

You can often find connection out of divisiveness, especially when you are willing to look for it. Remember, connection is the *given;* reality *is* connected. In the Quaker tradition, for example, having a group sit in silence is used as a way of coming to consensus. They hold that consensus *will* arise, because their tradition recognizes that there is interconnection. When you allow your egoic, personality-self to be still and quiet and not lead the way with thoughts and ideas, connection can more easily arise. Being with each other is connection in itself and through it you can find consensus or movement toward it.

ക്ക-ക്ക-ക്ക-ക്ക-ക്ക

Jeanne is a college professor with a young teenager. She is creative in music and arts and has been involved in spiritual philosophy and teachings for much of her adult life. As is not uncommon, her family does not directly share these interests, but are supportive of her endeavors.

"I have learned techniques that help me, but I find at times I return to prayers and blessings which help me feel better and more balanced. I think of this as cleansing myself and receiving angelic help and intervention. Can you comment on this?"

When you use familiar blessings and traditions, you are additionally supported, as these traditions have been energized by thousands of people over time. Embrace all the support within all the traditions. If you have tradition, a blessing, a prayer, a meditation, a ritual – whatever it is, there is space for this in your life, along with all the other avenues of insight and awareness. Angels, guides, animal totems and the like serve as powerful symbols or points of focus to connect to the All. Such images personalize the experience of the vastness and in that personification, work as a link or connecting point.

It is important, though, to not attach to the idea that one will be rescued by spirit or angelic intervention, as being rescued is a very different thing than asking for support. Asking of the All, "I don't know what to do and I'm going to call upon what I see as the energies to come, support me and be with me," references that you need help, but does not hold you as helpless. There can be forces in the universe that are much stronger, more powerful, that in fact, *could* rescue you. But waiting for angelic rescue is a very different energy than "I need help and I'm willing to *participate* in it." Your participation demonstrates your willingness to be accountable and responsible for yourself in a spiritually mature way.

"I feel different beings are helping us in another way, more than just aligning us. There is help that comes, often, when you ask for it. And sometimes when you don't."

When you say "not just aligning," remember that *aligning* doesn't mean straightening yourself out. It means when you are open, there is space for connection and links to be made – alignments. When you literally ask for help, you are sending an energetic signal calling for connection. You open *to* alignment as it may come, as opposed to *getting* specifically aligned according to some model. Again, the essential caveat is, do not *attach* to what you come to understand. Don't look in only one way or solidify your language or exalt the way you do discover. Acknowledge that you have your own way of thinking about something and that by the nature of things, still more can be learned. When you say, "To me, my favorite angel comes and straightens things out and it's really wonderful," you can stay open to further meaning and keep your attitude expansive by adding, "And I know it may be somewhat different than it seems to me." In this way, your favorite angel may reveal more to you; further experiences can occur. Such openness allows experience to shift and change; supporting that at another time you may be able to see further, wider, and deeper. When you make your interpretations solid and concrete, you close the door to further discovery.

"I read and learn of mystics and others who talk about ecstatic experiences and knowledge. I wonder if it is all illusion and misunderstanding or are they really experiencing these things."

Ecstatic experiences and knowledge exist and at the same time, can include illusion and misunderstanding. Individuals share what they have seen, what was available to them and how they understood the moment. Such sharing gives you an additional perspective to consider that can support you in allowing your *own* experiences. But it does not necessarily give you a map or directions to have the *same* experience. Nor do you need to orient yourself toward attaining experiences as described by others. Such experiences are open to everyone, not just mystics and teachers. You cannot get them by demand but you can open yourself to them. If one comes to you, be *with* it. Feel into it and from there allow yourself to come to *discernment* of your experience. Ask, "What is the core principle within this experience? I feel a moment of ecstatic bliss. Do I need to attach to it? Do I need to make sure I have it tomorrow? Can I own it and put it on the shelf?" Such questions will not diminish your experience, but will lead to it becoming an integrated aspect of your being, rather than a special spiritual event or attainment.

ക്കക്കക്ക

David is an artistic young man who works with computers. Feeling different, he found himself drawn to exploring different perspectives.

"I have had some profound experiences of receptivity, and am considering using this openness in some artistic or poetic way. I am open to suggestions how to use my empath nature in a way that could enhance my experience, make a contribution to the world and perhaps bring me some prosperity in the process."

Considering how to "use" your empath nature is putting the cart before the horse. This very nature will eventually lead you in how it can be best expressed. To open to discovering that way of expression, begin by turning your attention to feeling the essence of your own nature. Delight in the joy of your receptivity. Value the essence of yourself regardless of what you may come to do. The nature of bamboo is that it is a plant. The strength of the bamboo might *lead* us to make use of it, to do this or that with it. But the essence of a plant is to just be a plant, regardless of how it may come to be used. Doing emerges from essence.

Invite energy to your awareness by asking, "Can I bring the empath energy of my life into a focus? How can I bring it into a focus?" See what avenue of expression shows up. Allow and permit open receptivity and from that the work, the focus, the specifics will flow. It may be art; it may be something you have yet to imagine. At times people need to make *declarations*, as in, "I want to do empath art." Declarations are a way of amplifying energy. You are speaking to yourself before witnesses, setting out an idea and intent, hoping for support. Sometimes declarations never come to pass exactly as they are said, but usually when someone is moved to make a declaration, something does come present. A seed has been planted even when the blossoming is not as we imagine it. You've declared your impulse to create art and that is the beginning of your journey. Do not bind your creativity or limit your focus by requiring that your art be directly linked to prosperity. Are you truly saying, "I can't make art if I'm not sure how to market it and make money with it?" The language of ideas can funnel and limit possibility as well as expand your horizon. Consider adding to your intent your own version of "I am willing to release the outcome for the fullest good." Be willing to let life move you, as well as determining options and choices yourself.

᷒᷒᷒᷒᷒᷒᷒

James is a systems developer for a large corporation in a major city. He has been interested in being self-aware and working towards improving his life with that awareness for many years. He and his wife share this interest and try to live consciously from these principles.

"Earlier the group was talking about the dichotomies within the different teachings we work with. I had felt on very solid ground with certain perspectives, but now I see there is more fluidity to everything than I am comfortable with. There is the ideal that we're really all spirit and that we each have made the choice to become substantiated in this physical experience. The belief is that the ultimate goal of physical experience is to express love, joy and goodness; to radiate towards truth and express divine being in all its grand, glorious and beautiful aspects. And yet, I notice there is true vibrational pain and suffering here in the world that we have to deal with and manage. Why do some beliefs stand so strong and yet, seem so blatantly contrasted with our real life, physical and emotional experience?"

This ideal can be called transcendence and it is quite attractive indeed. It holds that if you just turn your eyes to another view, to spirit and beauty, then difficulty, strife or pain will not be present. Yet it is *all* here. There is not one ancient spiritual text that is beauty and light in its entirety. Every spiritual text and tradition has stories of destruction and re-creation; stories of battles and fights; of the day the sky turned black and all changed.

Like the images of angelic intervention, you must let yourself consider that there may be a broader view. The interconnections of life are so much more vast and complex than anything we can fully comprehend. Here, too, the ancient texts remind us that the full nature of god is ineffable, cannot be truly spoken or known. Yet it is natural for individuals to want to bring into their life an ideal where one would be able to supersede difficulty and challenge, pain and suffering. Such a perspective must be seen expansively, not concretely. Life is highly complex and interwoven in ways you cannot deconstruct or know.

Events do "crash" into your life. You can set intents and reach for alignments, but in the end you are part of this All in ways you cannot understand and especially, not control. Life may indeed, and very often does, take you *completely* where you don't want to go. Conscious intent is simply not the control device people want it to be. You may bring focus and intent to all you want, but you have to be open to the knowledge that whatever your focus may be, it may not be in your power to set events in motion or determine what will occur.

Where do you find yourself when your intent and vision do *not* happen? Where are you when the healthy person who did all the right things suddenly dies from an illness? Do you create a story about how that person didn't meditate on the third day of the month and therefore they *earned* their problem? Exalting the ideals of the power to control all too easily morphs into judgmental versions of good and bad, right and wrong. Or you can make up a more benign story where suffering is learning a cosmic lesson or that individuals offer themselves up for the good of others to balance karma and so on. All of these are meanings *given* to the situation. There may be *elements* of truth within such ideals, but primarily such perspectives serve as a defense from seeing the complexity of the truth, and acknowledging the limits of one's capacity to direct and control life.

Egoic consciousnesses, in form or not in form, cannot see or comprehend the vastness of the complex web of being. Bad things happen to good people and interestingly, these are very often vitality-filled change-points for individuals, cultures and realities. Again, paradox is a consistent experience of life. It is appropriate to *take*

149

meaning from things, but be willing to consider that your understanding is limited. Be willing to not know.

Further, it is a gift and blessing to consider that you do not *need* to know everything. You do not have the responsibility to completely fathom All There Is, the Vastness of Being, Ultimate Consciousness. Letting yourself be with the truth of each day is a great gift. In that gift, you will find the next step, one step at a time. The deep spiritual truth within life is simply that your life is not incumbent upon your knowledge or actions alone. As it is said, *you are not alone.* Remember what you *know* -- know beyond philosophy or psychology or spirituality -- that you are of the All. Not just part of, but expressions of the All in its vastness. All of the language we use to distill and delineate it can only hold bits and pieces. In any situation, you can say, "This is how it is. I'm going to accept that for now."

Your true choice always lies in how you chose to be with, respond to and flow with the what is of the moment. When you are standing there and don't know how to put one foot in front of the other, it is only the egoic mind that doesn't know how to move. You can stand in that unknowingness and declare, "I don't know what to do. I don't know how to be." In opening to *not* knowing, you *permit* the vastness of which you are to come present and help you to know.

As all the words have said to so many generations, through centuries and traditions, *ask and you shall be shown the way*. Most every person has had some moment when the way opens up, in one moment, for one step. You are part of this and it is available to and flowing through you. You can direct and control many aspects and details of life, but you simply will not control your entire life. It is not given to you to do so. Once you discover that you don't *have* to control your entire life, it can be a relief. Also, the control you value so is actually based on your past, your history and what you already know. What you will get by control alone is another version of what you already know, the life you've already lived.

In your willingness to respond to the invitation to wonder, you are open to that which you do not yet know. You are open to life taking you on a journey you cannot now imagine. You will also find strength and support to find your way through the worst of life, in ways you cannot know in advance. Life is expressed in myriad aspects no matter what certainty is wished for. The vitality of life is present in all its aspects. This is *living* spiritual awareness.

๙๙๙๙๙๙

One consistent note in the empath work
has been many individuals' sense of some
memory or knowing of an empath reality.

Such senses have been shared in private sessions and every workshop. Many people report dreams with vivid imagery. Others report locales that appear consistently in meditation. Still others share about knowledge that seems to just arise from an unknown place. On the following pages are questions and answers on the idea of empath realities.

During a workshop, Ken shared, **"As an empath, I am drawn to demand an energy flow from people and from life in a way that perhaps isn't native to this world.** I am interested in coping with the issues of empath nature, but I am not willing to relinquish my empathness in order to cope."

Learning about modulating or balancing your empath tendencies and capacities does not ask you to "relinquish your empathness." The emphasis is on recognizing that you have qualities that simply will *not* manifest here to a degree that matches your sense of them. Empaths often sense, recall and feel the capacity to connect in a flow, a closeness of connection that is a merging of thought, emotion, even physicality. Experiences of merging in daily life rarely match the intensity and completeness empaths sense as truly possible. Expecting to have this same connection is like comparing apples and oranges. By releasing such comparison, you can find ways to be more present as you are in the here and now. Releasing your idealized expectations can be the very movement that opens you to discovering the true depth of expression of empath energy in this realm of life.

Maryanne is in her 50's and has been working with these ideas of empath energy for many years. She has lived a life with a spiritual perspective and eventually became an inter-denominational minister. She also works as a manager in a large bookstore. The blend of speaking and sharing awareness in both occupations suits her very well.

"I wonder why a bunch of hyper-sensitive souls would choose to arrive at a moment when the input is overwhelming to everyone. I feel again and again that empaths came to save the world, like Mighty Mouse. What appeals to me about this image is that it gives the entire evolving process a purpose and meaning that feels supportive to me. I don't want to label myself or feel I have to save the world, but there is something about that feeling of purpose I want to keep or maybe conceptualize it in a broader way. So why do sensitive people come into this world with its constant barrage of news and the internet?"

You are taking meaning, creating meaning for yourself, from what being an empath feels like to you. In this case, you are using the meaning personally in a benign and positive way. But there are some cautions. What abounds so much in the current world are people who feel that *their* sense of meaning and purpose is tantamount. They feel driven to create restrictions; to limit and harm others who follow another sense of purpose. To balance meaning, remember to allow the articulation of your ideals to remain fluid, open to new language and understanding. It may be that your empath sense can indeed affect the wider world. It most certainly can have an effect on individuals in your personal world. Hold a sense of purpose, feel a sense of purpose, but be cautious not to elevate it or feel you have been given a cosmic mandate to take actions for the greater good.

"Once before you talked about considering a model of *exchange* between here and empath reality. I still feel at times as if I am bringing this particular kind of empathy to the less empathic, but I can feel judgment of others creeping in with that idea. I also find I am simply not clear as to the value of what 'here' is offering 'there.' You once said this connection and exchange could have a profound effect on our places of Home or Other. I would like to see this value, so I could equalize the relationship in my mind and feel an exchange."

These different realities have an *energetic* connection. There may literally be other realities, but the connections people experience are in energy and consciousness, not in physicality. The exchange between this reality and an empath collective reality has to do with *individuation.* The degree of individuation expressed here is a unique aspect of creativity. The impetus toward connection through communication acts as a unique creative spark that flourishes more in realities with individuation. This creativity is expressed not only in the arts, but in certain kinds of thinking; supporting paradigm shifts in thought and concept. A collective reality creates energy akin to the beauty and harmony of the acappella chorus. By its *blended* nature, it does not create the same kind of passion as the solo jazz scat singer, who follows the rhythm of her individual energy. Your very individuation and the variety a single note creates is what is exchanged. Just as you resonate with collective energy, the collective can resonate with *individual* energy and allow the vibration of the unique single being to expand its awareness of the possibilities of how one can be in life.

"**It is suggested again and again that empaths must learn to modulate their receptivity**. In the root place that empaths connect to, wouldn't one be out of balance by closing off receptivity through modulation? I thought we were bringing this very receptivity here?"

8

Sharing receptivity is very important to empaths, but there are distinct differences between an empath reality and this one. An empath realm would have a culture where principles of merging and transmuting are the nature of reality, with an energetic communication, without language or conceptualization per se. In this reality, understanding is inherently based on conceptualization. Symbols, images and language are used, rather than directly expressing or translating feelings. This reality is not an arena of direct energetic exchange. Empaths are required to deal with the continuing fact that words are limited in expressing the truth of what you sense, feel and know. In addition, words can also be manipulated to limit, alter and hide the truth. Language easily leads to misunderstanding, hidden agendas and double standards.

Communication in an empath reality is through direct energy exchange. You may now hold some capacity to *recognize* this kind of communication and to "speak" it with some, but direct energy communication is not very available. Thus, it is in accord to learn the language of your own reality. Awareness, discernment and modulation become key tools to participate and communicate. Do not *attach* to the ideas of empath roots. It is a misnomer that there is a distinct place "where empath energy comes from." Keep your models of understanding fluid.

"After personal sessions or workshops, I feel really wonderful and connected for awhile. Then I go through a terrible depression about how pointless everything is. I want to be back on my home planet."

You feel this especially after sessions and workshops because during them you sense and expand into "other" energy -- energy not only of this time and focus. Your recognition of otherness comes very present; feeling intensely tangible and visceral. Otherness is really a strong recognition of connection to the vastness and vitality of life. It is only "other" in that it tends to be felt more subtly in daily life, as it pulses quietly in the background, as your attention is required by the mundane. In an ongoing way, you connect to this expansive energy in dreams or meditative times. But after times of a more direct experience, such as a workshop where the intensity is amplified by your full attention and the group energy as well, the more subtle ways of connecting do not feel intense enough.

To amplify your own sense of recognition and connection you can create a ritualized, symbolic place to represent and hold this energy. Discover symbolic things that hold for you the energy of the deep knowing of the interconnection of all things, something that holds the quality of being at home in the All. This can be a stone, an image, or your own artwork. Perhaps your garden or sitting room can become your own sacred place where you bring together these things that represent grounding, support and again, connection. This place doesn't have to be isolated from others, but hold that it is a place for your personal renewal.

"I see a tendency for empaths to consciously compare this world with their sense of a home world. I have concluded that I myself come to quite an unfavorable comparison, feeling that this physical world just doesn't measure up."

The sense of a home world is a bit like "first love." The person seems perfect and all you want to do is think of them and be with them. The idealized image of home world is where you feel wholly accepted and naturally, you want to keep this sense of connection alive in your thoughts. You may also imagine, "If I just give up this connection here I will go back home." But this scenario is far from any possible truth. It is a symbol of the idealized feeling of 100% acceptance and connection.

Empath nature is present within you; it is not as if you were an alien sent to colonize earth, as appealing and pervasive as that imagery may be. The fact that you deeply experience your core essence as connected to otherwhere, does not mean that there is literally such a place or that you can directly connect with it physically or return there. The true task before you is to find an integral way to express this nature in your present reality.

A young boy declared, as a statement of himself to the world, "I am an Earth boy!" He said this with enthusiasm and joy at his discovery. No matter what energy one feels connected to, what root you feel as your own, what aspect you feel you are bringing present – what you all have in common is that you are "earth" boys and girls, earth men and women. You can share the energetic reality you touch into. Use your awareness to find the concepts and language of your nature. Follow the ultimate question, "I want to know how to think about who and what I am." Learn yourself. Know yourself.

We hold deep appreciation for the intimacy people have shared within this work, extending heartfelt thanks to all who have participated in the journey. The same appreciation and thanks is extended to you, the reader. Your attention adds to the energetic flow of the empath material and all that you may choose to share with others joins the flow of the recognition of empath consciousness. We speak to and for each other; learning with and from each other as well.

Spiritual maturity is found in your willingness to
bring your wisdom to bear, is found in your
willingness to see the truth and from there,
discover what you need to do, if anything.

Living your life within empath consciousness,
sharing and walking in empath energy,
can serve as a true example of another perspective,
another approach to living together
as a more connected whole.

CHAPTER EIGHT

Introduction to
GLOSSARY of PRINCIPLES and TOOLS

Let language be a tool of expansion.
Allow words the freedom to impart deep and varied meanings.
Do not use words to bind, but to support freedom of being.

Throughout this book various principles, tools, and techniques have been explored. Here, key points are brought together in an alphabetical glossary for easy reference and review.

In all things are core principles and from that,
myriad applications can emerge and evolve.
Open to that which has not yet been discovered.

In exploring the principles, align yourselves with the deep energy *within* the language of the principles. This will support, lead and guide you to open to that which you do not yet know and has not yet been discovered or realized.

Tools are reference points using language
to hold the principle of an idea or approach.
Find your personal interpretation or expression.

It is essential to discover your own language for these principles and approaches, tools and techniques. Cultivate conceptualizing in neutral phrases to allow your understanding to evolve broadly and expansively. Apply your own key-words, images or symbols to evoke personal meaning. Listen to your inner response and direction as you explore these ideas and apply your discernment to what is effective and useful in the moment. In the next moment, invite yourself to discover anew; to look with fresh eyes and ask still other questions.

Approaches to understanding ourselves in life
are always evolving and shifting.

Some ideas may serve you consistently; others are useful from time to time; still others, not at all. Discover your own variations on these themes and your own additions and alterations.

Conscious exploration of empath energy
is an exciting journey.

Let your life serve as a demonstration of new models and other ways to look at life. Open to fluid experiences of your receptivity. Allow yourself to evolve and mature into ease with your nature and what it brings to you and asks of you. The principles explored here can apply to many arenas of life. What is most exciting is the idea that you have chosen to enter into a living dialogue of integration; a living modality of an integral life. Here, spiritual awareness and spiritual principles come alive with vitality. Such principles are lived not only in meditation on Monday and church on Sunday, but in all of life. They are lived in moments like, "Right now I am in the kitchen and anger is rising up. What can I do with that?" The everyday is truly where we live with awareness.

This work on empath energy evolved from a dialogue of individuals who brought with them their perspectives and questions; their own answers and comments. Together they entered into unity with each other, sharing hearts, minds and essence. Dialogue is always a medium of exchange and sharing, even when it seems there is no agreement or mutual understanding. Know that when you share of yourself, the energy of your words and feelings exists and enters the flow of awareness, becoming available to those you may know and those you may never know.

ৰ্তিৰ্তিৰ্তিৰ্তিৰ্তিৰ্তিৰ্তি

GLOSSARY of PRINCIPLES and TOOLS

Acknowledgment/Acknowledging   Acknowledgment honors the "what is" in life. It does *not* mean agreement with, acceptance of, or capitulation to that which occurs. Rather, you are seeing the element of truth in a situation. "You are angry with me. I am insecure. I am afraid. I feel betrayed." These are simple statements *acknowledging* what you sense or see. Such a nod to the truth opens the way for shifts and change. Denial of the truth closes you off from discernment and usually sends you on a false, unclear path.

Acknowledging Your Fears   This is a simple technique built on the principle of *acknowledgment*. When you find yourself in conflict, understand that an aspect of yourself is fearful and uncomfortable. Acknowledge the fear by making a statement to yourself about the fear. "I acknowledge I am very uncomfortable with the idea of doing something that might be challenging for my partner." Fear usually eases in intensity when it is seen and acknowledged. But be clear, you are not trying to convince yourself of any specific intent or action. Rather, you are trying to simply find words that echo the *truth* of your feelings. Actions to overcome or shift the fears will arise in their own time.

All There Is/the All   This is the core principle of this sharing. All There Is and the All point to the vast consciousness of being of which individuals are expressions, and that is always present and expressing through life itself.

Allowing and Permitting Another core principle based in the recognition of the All and the interconnection of all things. In this, you can see there are times that your direct will, intent or coercion of a situation is the not the aligned path. Be open to allowing and permitting yourself at times to step back from the conscious approach, and invite the All to show you a way, reveal an insight, bring more information or make a connection.

Aspects The idea of aspects of the personality useful in seeing more clearly the paradoxical nature of life. This model also can help one *dis-identify* with those aspects that limit you, binding you to fears and pain from the past. There are patterns that seem to be paradoxical; needs and wants that push and pull in different and opposite directions at the same time. Aspects represent individual pieces that develop at different times and from varied events and causes. These aspects feel disconnected and separate and do not operate in an integrated way. When you can allow and accept that there may always be such pushing and pulling and disconnected compartments, you can see these separate aspects as emotional states that *interact* with the whole of you. Consider yourself as part of a great collage, a grand assemblage. See the varied and diverse aspects of life as an expression of wholeness evolving from the complex. See your self reflecting the myriad threads of the web of interconnection and being a part of the grand mosaic.

Awareness, Felt-Awareness, Discerning-Awareness

These terms point to a knowing system that is broader and less defined than learned empirical knowledge or skills. The principle is rooted in the idea that you are connected to All There Is. Through that connection, you can open to receive information and comprehension and discover knowledge through the seemingly indirect process of opening to receptivity. This type of knowing can, at times, be experienced as a completely different way of coming to awareness. At other times, it works with and enhances learned knowledge. Consider it as another capacity available to work with the fullness of you.

Being   In simple terms, this reflects the quality of having life. In a broader context, being refers to the deep essence of life, the place of interconnection with All There Is. This depth of connection informs your personality and sense of self and can lead you to awareness beyond the conscious mind.

Box on the Shelf   This technique is helpful for situations you want closure with, cannot get clear about or need more information, time and distance from. Sit quietly, think about and feel into what you wish to shift or become integrated. Frame your intent about the situation. Write down a reference to the situation; a description, a person's name or whatever symbolizes the situation for you. Simply place the paper in a box with a lid and *literally* put it away on a shelf. You are energizing your awareness by making it symbolic and anchoring your intention with the direct physical action of writing and literally putting it away from your thoughts. This tool correlates well with Time-Limit/Time-Opening.

Cards on the Table   Your willingness to place your cards on the table brings clarity by expressing the truth of your feelings, senses, etc. Ask, "What do I want? What do I feel? What don't I know?" Allow yourself to hear what arises and just "pops up" in response to your inquiry. Separate a need to take *action* from the act of *inquiry*. Let the information settle until a true discernment evolves. Allow yourself to put the truth on the table when sharing with others as well. The caveat in this case is that you cannot control the outcome of such sharing. You may or may not be understood as you would like. Clear sharing is effective when you are truly aligned to releasing the outcome and are in an emotional place where you can accept responses you may not want or expect. Before you bring your "truth" to another for their response, examine deeply whether what is here is *your* own question to answer or your own desire to fill.

Cloaking   Empaths must often cope with receiving too much input. Cloaking is a useful tool to manage what is received. Picture what allows you to feel able to be open and permeable to a degree that is comfortable to you. You can create an image of a literal cloak, a waterfall or web of energy that serves as a filter of input received. Such symbols create a conscious symbol of desire to modulate the energy flow you receive.

Cocoons   In early childhood, feelings, fears, hurts or concerns get cocooned, becoming encapsulated emotions that have not been explored or transmuted and are nested within the psyche. When you discover your "buttons," your places of reaction, consider that they are linked to unexplored cocoons of energy and work toward opening and understanding what may lie within.

Conditioning   This refers to the myriad aspects of living that impact and affect you, creating reactions and responses. Many of these reactions become subconscious, no longer clearly linked to their first impetus and responding to situations which in some way, echo or resonate with the early experience. Knowing that everyone has some conditioned responses opens your awareness to uncovering early roots of these responses and looking at them anew. At other times, knowing the principle that there is this force at work allows you to find ways to simply deal with your responses.

Discerning Awareness   Awareness and attention are linked with conscious knowledge and considerations, bringing your discernment to the situation. Discernment also involves the quality of being able to see that which is not typical or overtly evident.

Ebb and Flow   Life is a continuing movement. Ebb can be experienced as times of low energy and slow movement, but the slowness is more like an in-breath, a time and space of quietness and receptivity, collecting energy for the next out-breath. Flow reflects the coalescing and synthesizing of that which has been received and is then expressed in movement and action. Acknow- ledging that life is not a steady progression allows you to work with the natural active and inactive aspects of energy.

Empath DNA   Key words of a model considering empath nature as innate and an integral part of your basic emotional-biophysical system. The model supports you in accepting the embedded nature of empath qualities, rather than seeing sensitivity, for example, as something to overcome.

Empath Energy   The empath energy system is of a higher, deeper velocity and intensity than the physical energy of the body. You must work *with* the physical and use your mind as the guardian to set up structures that support the physical. Structures and boundaries support expressing empath nature in a comfortable and blossoming way.

Empath Nature   A field of strong receptivity and sensitivity operating as an innate, autonomic emotional-biophysical energy system.

Empath Shame   Empaths carry an innate, powerful desire to respond, to transmute, or to change certain energies and when they cannot, they feel ashamed, as if they failed and are out of integrity.

Empirical History of Awareness   As you discover and understand, you create a history of awareness, built upon your own observations. You can use this history to refine your understanding of tools and techniques, to establish a place of reference and context for reactions and feelings and so on.

Energy   Energy is the dynamic quantity in life imbued with the capacity of action. It is the current of life that flows through all of us and all things; a vitality that can ebb and flow. Energy is experienced as feelings and emotions. Energy represents connection – within ourselves, between people, with cultures and places. Energy can be seen as affinity and/or resonance.

Energy Dance/ Energy Song   This approach invites you to allow energy to move through you in a non-structured way. Allow your body to move to music in a way that simply allows the energy to flow. Allow your voice to give rise to music, tones and singing in a similar manner. Each dance or song will have its own flow and will find its own completion.

Gathering Basket   This technique is based upon allowing and permitting. When you are exploring specific issues, considering new opportunities and changes, you can set up a gathering basket as a way to allow and permit information, ideas, leads and links to come present. Gather your questions or desires to yourself and release them to the All. You may want to write them down and place them in a basket or whatever container you choose. Without censorship, gather in all that comes to you. Postcards, images that catch your eye, a feather you find while walking, a comment or quote from a friend. There is an actual flow to this receiving process. When it ebbs, sit with your basket and see what associations, connections and ideas arise. Linking tangible items to ideas and thoughts amplifies receptive energy and your response to it.

Gestalt   Referring to deep inner *knowing*; when knowledge and awareness come together and are felt as a powerful whole. By definition, gestalt is seen as a configuration so integrated it is seen and recognized as a whole, with properties more than the sum of its parts.

Heart Bear   A technique to link you to the childhood comfort and trust of a beloved Teddy Bear. Find a soft, stuffed animal that appeals to you. Embrace the bear, holding the intent that you are

168

going to allow release of emotions. Visualize the bear as caring, comforting and able to absorb and transmute any and all emotion. Let yourself drift with this feeling and allow whatever response may arise. This approach sometimes takes a bit of time. Be giving and gentle with yourself. Many people report strong releases of energy, including crying, deep sobs and sadness. The Heart Bear unconditionally accepts the energy and offers comfort in return.

History of Awareness *– see Empirical History of Awareness*

Language Bridges Choose words and phrases that serve as a bridge to link to another person and truly share ideas and concepts. Language bridges hold the essence of a situation and serve as an archetype of one's intent. Words are selected with the intent to *allow* people to shift rather than demanding agreement. Using neutral language enhances the process. Language bridges are also used to communicate a set position in a way that the other person may accept your feelings, and give at least a begrudging yes. It may not be wholehearted, but a begrudged yes is agreement on some level.

Integral/Integration This principle holds that to live with more connection within the aliveness of life, you can lead yourself toward integration of your varied aspects, understandings, reactions, responses, and realities. Such integration is an active, mutable, flowing *process*, akin to gears meeting and meshing, not a static moment merging the varied into a singular understanding. Operating with an integral perspective allows you to move with the ups, downs, ins and outs of the moving energy systems of which life is made. In this way, all is embraced and included, with nothing excluded. You do not merely transcend and go beyond where you have been. As you include and integrate where you have been, you grow *further*.

Interconnection of All Things – *also see All, Unity, Vastness*

The inherent quality of interconnection reminds us of the inter-relatedness and codependence of life, some of which we can recognize; other facets we can only sense or surmise.

Inquiry   A tool of awareness in which you ask questions of yourself, inquire into your reactions and responses, explore your understanding and so on. Inquiry can be done in dialogue with other people, can arise through journaling and can be used in conjunction with body work and movement practices, such as yoga and tai chi.

Models and Questioning the Models   Culture uses language to define and delineate reality. Such definitions or models are constructs to understand a concept, an action or principle. Remember that *all* understandings are models reflecting knowledge from a certain perspective at a given moment. To allow awareness in your life, you have to consciously and consistently question the models. Do not let your vocabulary solidify or your descriptions set limits. Do not let yesterday's comprehension determine today's understanding without question or consideration.

Neutral Language   You can support yourself emotionally and gain understanding through using language that describes "what is" in neutral terms. You can say, "Am I depressed?" or more *neutrally*, ask, "Am I feeling fatigued and tired?" "Depressed" holds an array of subjective meanings. "Tired" describes a literal state. The neutral state supports broader models of understanding and diffuses emotional reactions and attachments to certain words.

Observer/Witness   It is useful to develop an observer aspect of your mind. The observer quality usually grows concurrently with self-inquiry and awareness. The observer or witness sits in the background, as it were, somewhat disengaged from emotional reactions and responses. At times we are compelled by conditioning to react and take action that we know may not be the best course. The observer helps us grow in understanding. Deeper understanding supports the possibility of change in your responses and actions.

Otherwhere/Otherwhen   Referring to the sense that one is connected to another place, realm, dimension or time in addition to current physical reality. Many empaths express a deep feeling of such a connection.

Paradox   Paradox arises when customary understanding leads to where seemingly opposite senses, feelings, wants and desires are true and exists at the same time. Models of thinking lead to the idea that situations can resolve into a single point of truth. Considering paradox in your life opens your awareness to finding ways to acknowledge the existence of such contradiction and through that, find ways to balance and work with it.

Releasing the Outcome   An attitude brought to bear particularly with intent and goals. It is rooted in the principle that as individuals we cannot know all that is involved with a situation. You may want to hold a specific focus or goal, but by releasing the outcome, you allow your focus to be permeable and expansive; open to allowing change and possibility you had not yet considered.

Pause for Discernment   Cultivate your willing-ness to "pause for discernment." Invite clarity about a situation, asking, "Is this what is most aligned for me at this time? Am I responding to that which I don't fully understand?" Discernment is achieved through the broadness of sensing-awareness in concert with conscious awareness. Your conscious awareness can recognize the moment to pause, interrupting or stopping the mind-stream of "I know." In that pause, you open to awareness that flows from within and without. This allows the opportunity to sense or realize that which is more expansive than learned ideas and responses alone. The pause also opens you more fully to alignment with the flow of All There Is.

Renewal Zones   Actions and situations that refresh and revitalize your emotional and physical energy and well-being. Renewal Zones are created by recognizing what does renew you and establishing and ritualizing certain routines to support that experience; as an example, taking one evening a week to yourself.

Resonate   Recognizing and matching vibration and energy; feeling connected to a person, idea, situation, etc. This connection is often experienced as intense and enriching.

Self-Inquiry - *see Inquiry*

Speaking on the Wind At times you may feel you are not understood or invited to voice your sense of a situation. You can try to communicate through the vast interconnection of all things. You can speak to the essence of another, sharing your feelings while releasing your image of the outcome. Offer your willingness to see what alignments may evolve; trust in the alignments of the All. Find an open, receptive time for you in quiet space. Clear the personality mind and begin to allow yourself to speak from your "heart." Heart energy represents the sensing awareness that recognizes the connection of the All. It is not directed or compelled by our egoic patterns and wounds. Share from your heart to their heart; from your fullest self to their fullest self. Interesting resolutions and realignments emerge from this energetic sharing that you may not have consciously envisioned.

Subconscious - *see Unconscious* Elements or aspects that you may have sensed or recognized but which have become less conscious and available to your conscious mind.

Symbols Language, images and concrete items that represent points of reference and focus. They are often used to anchor attention and to initiate change.

Time-Limit/Time-Opening This approach is useful for allowing change, especially when you are unclear about your choice of action. When the path is not clear, consider that perhaps all the information required may not have yet coalesced into useful clarity.

You can then decide to take *no* action at this time by feeling into the situation, as in, "For now I won't decide about this and I'll look again at the situation in a month." Let the actual timing arise on its own. The object is to engage the *conscious* mind with a time-limit in support of inner permission to *not* consider the situation *directly* until the arbitrary time, which in turn, can create what we call a time-opening. What is "opened" is the possibility of considering in less conscious ways. By separating your feelings from a requirement of action, you can explore a situation, without the pressure of taking immediate action. This approach works well with the Box on the Shelf tool.

Tool Box   Consider the principles, concepts and techniques you learn and discover as part of your tool box of awareness. Rather than a list of rules, you have tools *available* for the various issues, tasks or focuses that arise in life. Pause in the moment and ask, "What would best serve here?" From that pause, concepts and principles garnered through your empirical history of awareness will arise and support you in the next step.

Tool of Reference   Reference is a way to place feelings and worries in a *context* by asking questions about them to help disengage from your immediate reaction. Essentially you are asking, "When I feel like this, what does it remind me of?" Understanding that you operate from sub-text contexts gives you a platform to become an observer of your responses. From this witness place, you may be able to make more considered choices or wait for reactions to settle before you take any actual action.

Transduce/Translate/Transmute   A triad of key words that represent the core capacities available to empaths to manage energy received.

Transducing Energy   Transducing refers to a specific way of changing energy received or sensed, i.e., modulating or stepping down the felt impact of the vibration. The word points toward an *energetic* process, initiated by conscious intent.

Translating Energy   Translation serves as a key principle in communicating the quality of energy received. Empaths can find more concrete language or actions to express that which they sensed in less tangible ways. Translation includes sharing your sensings with others and helping others articulate their own sensing.

Transmuting Energy   Transmuting or changing energy by bringing conscious focus toward *allowing* energy received to be acknowledged, expressed and to change. The empath does not create changes directly, but opens to the capacity to use your intent as an initiator, in which you ask for energy to be released through you and changed in the movement of the All. Thus, fearful energy can be offered to transmutation and then released from the body.

Treat The Symptom   Working with awareness, you often feel *every* aspect should be explored and completely understood, but you simply cannot deconstruct every element that affects you. Life has stress and the body does react to it. Sometimes it is appropriate to simply treat the symptom: get a cup of tea, read a novel, watch a movie. Take a deep breath, sit on the deck or go for a walk. Put a shield of energy around you; have a massage; take an action to balance and alleviate stress. If an unresolved issue lies at the heart of your response, it will certainly come again to be examined. Treat the symptom and follow up with deeper inquiry at another time.

Unconscious – *see Subconscious* Elements or aspects that are deeply unavailable to your conscious mind.

Vastness A term that points toward to the All of life and the Interconnection of All Things.

Witness – *see Observer/Witness*

What Is This phrase refers to the truth of the present moment; considering and accepting how something truly is. It is difficult to work with awareness when you look through the lens of your ideals and ideas of how things are, rather than truly allowing the recognition of what actually is.

Whole/Wholeness Referring to a spiritual quality of completeness and acceptance that encompasses all the seemingly paradoxical nature of oneself and life

DANCERS BETWEEN REALMS

Perhaps you feel as a traveler, at times alone and disconnected. Yet you sense a "Home" place. However you may sense it, you carry it with you. Tenderly in your heart, deeply in your soul, you carry Connection. Know there is always a way to be There and always a way to be Here in harmony and balance.

You are a dancer between realms and dancers always hear and feel the music. In the rhythm of the music of empath nature and human nature there is a most glorious dance that evolves day by day. You are part of this evolving symphony. Each note matters and when those notes are not present, they are missed.

Appreciate this pioneer energy you carry in your glorious physical self and bring new ways of expressing empath energy. Feel the vitality of being in the physical with the bubbling energy of individuality. Feel the intensity of having collective energy touching into and flowing through a single being. Feel the excitement of aware living and an integral life. Sense the coming evolution of yourself and those who may evolve with you and from you, as you are part of an energetic heredity.

Appreciate yourself. Appreciate who you are now and where you have come from. Appreciate who you are becoming as you move toward blossoming and flourishing.

ACKNOWLEDGMENTS

Heartfelt thanks and appreciation are extended to all who have shared their experiences and their willingness to discover another perspective in the ongoing exploration of empath energy.

Deepest appreciation and a passionate thank you to HELEN SELINE for her incredible support in bringing this book into being. Her collaborative energy was the initiating force. She brought her attention and skill to editing the original source text, to providing a way to develop a text database, to editing the final book and continually supporting me personally through all the ups and downs, ebbs and flows, seeming stuck places and frustration of bringing this book into being. Her presence in my life is a great gift.

GAY OSBORNE supported the empath work for years on end, sharing personally, supporting workshops, having many sessions transcribed and after the loss of disks, providing her own archive copies of a wealth of material.

LESLIE FRANCE was invaluable in helping organize the source material by working with me to design a searchable database. Leslie is our graphics designer, creating the cover layout and design and graciously provided support and answers to technical questions innumerable times.

Deb Booth provided the cover image, sharing her wonderful photography with openness, enthusiasm and her special brand of zest. Many images were explored until "Energy Flow" spoke to us all.

Words cannot hold my deep appreciation for my husband, **Dennis Galumbeck**, who is the continuing support in my life. His quiet patience stood by and 'held down the fort' as I spent many hours sequestered in my office. His green thumb creates lovely gardens inside and out for retreat and renewal. And he knows when to tell me to stop working and whisk me off to dinner in a favorite restaurant.

Extraordinary thanks to **Dennis, Helen** and **Nora Harris** for serving as the primary editing team.

Special **T**hanks also to **Alexander Fitzhugh, April McGuigan, Benn Kobb, Cat McClannan, Catherine Klingenberg, Ellyn Dye. Forest Jones, Jane Batt, Jim Marian, Justin X. Frank, Laura EnglishJones, Lea Mesner, Lynn Koiner, Michael Gritz, Sandy Sawmelle, Steve T.H. Sawmelle, Steven Iordanous, Susan Glover, Teresa Rogovsky, Terri Thomas** and other contributors not named here. You each have shared and given so much in so many ways and at many times. Your presence and being is deeply appreciated.

And a **S**pecial **D**edication to **Patricia Serino** and **Christian Crislip**. They were with us at the beginning of the exploration of empath energy. They are always missed, but their sharing and energy continue to be intertwined with the empath material.

❦❦❦❦❦❦

Dancers Between Realms text on page 175 was excerpted from the closing remarks to an empath workshop in 1997.

ABOUT THE AUTHOR

This book is collaboration in so many ways. The participants in workshops and individual sessions have shared questions, insights and their lives with each other, and now with you. The work itself is a unique collaboration between Elisabeth Fitzhugh and the expansive consciousness referred to as the Orion group.

We understand Orion to be an expression of the intelligent consciousness of which we are all aspects. Consider that you are more than your physical body, and thus can perceive and know more than the readily available physical world. Consider that you exist in a flow of intelligent consciousness you can connect with. Consider a process whereby a person allows the opening of inner pathways or channels to link with such a connection and allow it to express through and with you. This is the Orion experience -- an expansive consciousness expressing through Elisabeth Fitzhugh. The channeling process seems intriguing, but more importantly, Orion has consistently presented a non-dogmatic, inspiring view of reality, with dynamically useful and applicable information oriented toward evoking your own recognition and resonance with expanded awareness.

Orion offers a resonance to support your capacity to transcend to further awareness, as you also embrace and *include y*our life's journey so far. Orion always shares as an interaction and exchange of equal value between realms of awareness. "Orion" is a symbolic name given to the group, representing interaction and friendship between realms.

Orion presents their work as an interactive collaboration. They work with Elisabeth as part of the group, aspects of her life at times inform their attention and focus; participants' questions and comments bring still further elements of focus, and new language and articulations emerge from these interactions.

Elisabeth has been sharing the Orion experience for over twenty years. Long attracted to understanding the nature of things, Elisabeth came to her exploration of spiritual awareness through  studies in psychology, anthropology and art. Experiences during the in-retreat Gateway Voyage™ program at the Robert Monroe Institute in Faber, Virginia in 1982, led to her work with Orion and today she is in her second decade of sharing this unique perspective.

Elisabeth is a cognizant channel. When the connection with Orion came fully present in 1983, her willingness to be present in the work supported Orion's focus of conscious interaction between realms of being. Elisabeth always shares that this inner decision, the willingness to be cognizant in the receptive mode, was a grand gift. Being immersed in all the Orion material and seeing all the variations of the theme is like being in the 'ultimate graduate course' – an ongoing, always fresh exploration of the vastness of reality.

The Orion work was centered in Washington, DC for many years. The Washington, DC area continues to be an anchor place for Orion workshops and presentations. Elisabeth now lives in the small city of Waynesboro, Virginia in the beautiful Shenandoah Valley.

We invite you to consider our perspective.
You are asked not to 'believe', but to consider.
Your innate wisdom will guide you
to accept only that which is aligned to you.
Allow yourself the gift of exploration.

Orion

If you are drawn to know more about Empath Energy and
other elements of the work with the Orion consciousness,
please visit us at

w w w . o r i o n w i s d o m . u s

Also by the author –
The Orion Material –
Perspectives of Awareness

Box 1154
Waynesboro, Virginia 22980 USA
www.synchronicitypress.com

Synchronicity –
the sense of significance beyond chance